Advanced
Airgun Hunting

A Guide to Equipment, Shooting Techniques and Training

Advanced
Airgun Hunting

A Guide to Equipment, Shooting Techniques and Training

John Bezzant

The Crowood Press

First published in 2011 by
The Crowood Press Ltd
Ramsbury, Marlborough
Wiltshire SN8 2HR

www.crowood.com

British Library Cataloguing-in-Publication Data
A catalogue record for this book is available from the British Library.

ISBN 978 1 84797 294 1

Acknowledgements
The author would like to thank Theoben Rifles and Tony Gibson of Hawke Optics
for their assistance with the preparation of this book.

Typeset by Servis Filmsetting Ltd, Stockport, Cheshire

Printed and bound in India by Replika Press Pvt Ltd

Contents

Introduction

As you will have gathered from the title of this book, it is about advanced airgun hunting; but what exactly do I mean by that? Well, quite simply, I mean pushing the sport to the very limits of its capabilities, with regard to the range at which quarry is engaged. Under normal circumstances there is no justification for the airgun shooter to take a shot at anything beyond 35yd, and even this distance should only be considered by very accomplished marksmen: for most the range for humane shooting will not exceed 30yd.

However, when the very best equipment in the airgun world is combined with the highest standards of marksmanship, then that range can be dramatically increased to 40 or 45yd. You will note the statement, 'when the best equipment is linked with the best marksmanship', as it takes both equipment and marksmanship to make up the correct equation for long-range shooting. You can spend £1000 on a state-of-the-art PCP air rifle, then mount a £500 scope on top of it, but that does not make you a long-range sharpshooter – it simply means that you have the equipment to do the job. Unless you are willing to spend hundreds of hours on the range in order to acquire the required level of marksmanship for long-range shooting, then the rifle and scope, though capable enough for the job, will be totally useless.

In this book you will find a training schedule for advanced marksmanship, structured in a similar way to the training programmes used by the military to train snipers. It takes the military just over two months of constant daily instruction to create a sniper,

which, in itself, tells you the amount of investment, in terms of the time required, to achieve advanced levels of marksmanship. If you are not willing to put in that kind of effort, then you are morally obliged not to engage in the application of long range shots at live targets, as the result is going to be a guaranteed injury to a living thing, which is not acceptable.

Any airgun hunter who does not hold to the creed of slaying the quarry with the first shot, has no right to own an air weapon. Yes, there are the odd occasions when an injury occurs due to a mistake, a misjudgement, or movement of the quarry at the moment the shot is released, but such occasions should be rare. Every possible measure should be taken to make sure they do not occur and, when it comes to long-range shooting, that means training yourself on the range for up to 150 hours. That seems like an awful lot of time – and indeed it is – but the plain fact of the matter is that long-range marksmanship is a highly advanced skill and not something that will just fall into your lap. If you want to become a long-range airgun sharpshooter, then prepare yourself for a great deal of study and even more work.

The first thing that you are going to require is a shooting range measuring 50yd. My other airgun book *Air Rifle Shooting for Pest Control and Rabbiting* shows you how to build a target range. If you do not know how to build a safe range, consult my other book and you will have all the information that you require. Advanced airgun hunting, as well as engaging live targets at long range, includes a number of other subjects that require the shooter to develop an advanced level of skill. Such subjects include:

- The use of a chronograph.
- The use of night vision equipment.
- The precision alignment of the scope, with the bore of the rifle it is mounted to.
- A detailed understanding of scope and rifle mechanics.
- The fine-tuning of hunting rifles for accuracy.

This list is a basic one, and by no means encompasses all the subjects that the advanced airgun hunter must have a detailed grasp of. In order to achieve the standards required for advanced airgun marksmanship, you are going to have to spend six months or more studying and practising, as you hone your knowledge and skills to the required level.

The prospect of spending so much time developing your air gun skills should not put you off, but should excite you, because, once you have completed this period of disciplined self-training, you will take your shooting to a much higher level than you ever imagined was possible.

You will find many exercises in this book that have been very carefully designed to aid the reader to develop their skills; if you cheat on these exercises the only person you cheat is yourself. The exercises in this book will only work if you give them 100 per cent. The advanced airgun marksman is, above all else, committed to excellence and pursues it with dedication. Without this kind of drive and determination, your marksmanship will always be moderate and you will never be able to engage live targets past 30yd.

Chapter 1
The Long-Range Hunting Air Rifle

CHAPTER OBJECTIVES

The chapter objectives are divided into two categories:

Knowledge:

This refers to the academic understanding that you should have acquired by the time you reach the end of the chapter.

Practical Ability:

This refers to the practical skills that you need to develop by carrying out the exercises in the chapter.

KNOWLEDGE

This chapter should provide you with a clear understanding in three areas:

1 You should be able to explain what is meant by the term 'precision hunting rifle' and list the components that are needed to manufacture such a rifle.
2 You should be able to explain how the major components of a precision hunting rifle work, with a particular emphasis on their influence in relation to the weapon's accuracy and power output.
3 You should have an academic understanding of why a precision hunting rifle needs to be set up in a bespoke manner, designed to the particular characteristics of the shooter. You should also have an understanding of why precision maintenance is required.

PRACTICAL ABILITY

Following the exercises laid down in this chapter you should be able to carry out the following practical tasks:

1 You should be able to set the stock and trigger, in order to achieve optimum performance from you precision hunting rifle.
2 You should be able to carry out a partial strip down of your rifle, to prepare it for essential maintenance.
3 You should be able to carry out the routine servicing that your rifle requires.

Time Period Required To Acquire These Practical skills:

Ten to fifteen hours, depending on existing levels of ability.

A SUITABLE WEAPON FOR LONG RANGE SHOOTING

The rifles featured in this book are all Theoben's, which I consider to be the best hunting air rifles in the world; all the instructions for maintenance and fine-tuning are therefore specific to Theoben rifles, however the principles are applicable to all rifles, whatever their make.

In this chapter I present very specific guidance regarding the strip down and maintenance of Theoben weapons. If, however, you choose to use another make of rifle, you must carry out intensive levels of research on the internet, or using books and magazines, to acquire information on how to fine-tune and maintain your weapon to the same level as laid down for the Theoben rifles. There is only sufficient room in this book to cover one rifle to the required depth for long range hunting and, for that reason, I have chosen to work with Theoben, the pioneers of the modern precision long-range hunting air rifle.

THE PRECISION MADE AIR RIFLE

Just as you will never break the world land speed record in a Reliant Robin, you will not succeed at engaging long-range targets with just any old air rifle. If you have ever flicked through the *Gun Mart* or a similar publication, you may have noticed that nearly all the field target and match air rifles advertised carry a substantial price tag. This is simply because they are machined to extremely high levels of precision and it is this attention to fine detail that makes the weapons pinpoint-accurate. If precise engineering is the key to producing an accurate weapon for a target discipline, it is also the key criterion for producing a supremely accurate hunting weapon.

The first thing that you need to accept about precision engineering is that it does not come cheap; precision, by its very nature, is a time-consuming undertaking and it generally requires the hand operating of machinery by craftsmen. Cheap, mass-produced air rifles are plentiful in number and, although they have their uses, long-range shooting is not one of them. When it comes to precision engineering British airgun manufacturers are the world leaders; the two most accomplished and skilled manufacturers in this field being Theoben and Daystate.

One dictionary definition of precision is: being exactly what is called for or needed – neither more nor less. That is what you are looking for in a long-range hunting air rifle: a weapon that is exactly what is called for, being neither more nor less. Under-engineering will mean the weapon cannot achieve the accurate delivery of a projectile

at range, whilst over-engineering will make it too complex and unreliable for the field. This is one of the main reasons why hunters do not go hunting with target rifles; the other reason is that target rifles tend to be a bit too heavy for the field.

When precision engineering is used to manufacture an air rifle, the weapon produced will have components that align almost perfectly to within acute tolerances; this means that the delivery and passage of air through the rifle's ports will be smooth. The ports are the pathways down which the air travels from reservoir to breech. Any roughness in these tiny passages will cause turbulence that will deliver a disturbed charge of air into the pellet's skirt, giving it a violent shove, rather than a measured push into flight.

It is therefore common sense that, the smoother and less disturbed the pellet's journey down the barrel and its exit from it, the better it will travel. The benefit of precision engineering when it comes to the production of the moving parts of a weapon means that they will all move very cleanly, with no chaffing or stiffness; the trigger and hammer exhibiting a very light, yet positive, touch. The hammer is the part responsible for releasing the charge of air measured by the regulator.

You want the moving parts of the gun to operate with a supreme degree of ease and gentleness because, the less movement created by the moving parts, the less the disturbance the gun offers to the shooter. In other words, the less a gun moves when it discharges, the easier it is to maintain its line of fire on the mark. A well-engineered gun, produced by a skilled gunsmith using a high degree of precision, is essential to achieve long-range shots. Precision-made weapons will also have better seals, because the housings into which these seals fit are machined to a higher tolerance level; better-fitting seals mean that none of the air released from the regulator will escape on its way to the breach, thus the delivery of power will remain consistent from shot to shot. Consistency is the foundation stone on

*The Theoben
Tactical precision
long-range hunting
rifle.*

which accuracy is built and very few airguns are truly consistent.

Another major factor that affects accuracy is the machining of the choke at the muzzle end of the barrel. The choke is a narrowing of the barrel designed to provide a very gentle, vice-like effect on the pellet. The aim is to squeeze each and every pellet to the same size, ensuring that they are all uniform, and therefore guaranteeing that all the pellets fired from the gun behave in the same fashion, making ultra-consistent shot placement achievable. Theoben pay particular attention to the choking of every barrel, performing the task by hand to an exceptionally fine degree of tolerance to ensure maximum consistency; it is this attention to fine detail that makes the precision-made air rifle such a phenomenal weapon.

The objective of this book will be to produce a 12mm consistent grouping at 40yd, which is not something that can be achieved by every air rifle, but only those that are precision-engineered. Having handled a very wide selection of weapons, I believe there are only a handful of guns that I would term precision-engineered. There are lots of well-made, accurate weapons that perform superbly out to 30yd, but that is the limit of their ability when it comes to pushing the sport to the very edge of its capabilities. In those situations a good gun, or even a very good gun, is just not sufficient – only the best will do.

There are only a handful of hunting rifles in a league of their own and in this chapter I will introduce you to one of the very best. We will examine them in significant depth to demonstrate the kind of intimate knowledge the advanced airgun hunter must have of their weapon, in order to engage in long range shots at live quarry.

Simply knowing how to disengage the safety, load the magazine and charge the air reservoir, is by no means sufficient knowledge to allow the hunter to engage long-range live targets – you will also have to know exactly how much power your rifle is capable of delivering at ranges from 20 to 40yd. The airgun hunter has a very small amount of power to play with: just 12ft/lb compared to the minimum 1000ft/lb a bullet gun is able to produce. We therefore have to know exactly, not roughly, what velocity the rifle is exhibiting, right across the full spectrum of ranges at which the advanced airgun hunter will be operating. This is not as difficult as it sounds; it just takes time, perseverance and an electronic measuring device called a chronograph.

You will also need to know how to carry out a partial strip down of the weapon, how to adjust the trigger, how to clean the barrel and how to recognize faults. You will need to have a very clear picture of the external ballistic behaviour exhibited by pellets propelled from the rifle's muzzle. The advanced airgunner must have a very intimate knowledge of the weapon they are using if they wish to be both successful and humane in the taking of quarry.

SPRING GUNS VERSUS PCPs

You will not find any spring or gas ram rifles in this section on long-range hunting rifles and that is simply because, good as some of them are, the best of them cannot match the accuracy offered by a precision-made PCP. The reason for this is quite simple: spring guns and gas ram guns move when fired and exhibit recoil of a very challenging nature, whereas PCPs do not move to any perceptible degree. Common sense will tell you that; the less a rifle moves during the discharge of its projectile, the more accurate it will be.

Some of the very best airgun marksmen in the country can get a spring or gas ram gun to perform out to 40yd, but even these very skilled shots will acknowledge that the more reliable and accurate weapon, and the one capable of the tightest groups at long range, is the PCP, winning the competition over spring or gas ram guns, hands down. Not only do PCPs not move, they can also deliver a much smoother and more finely measured charge of air to the breech than can be achieved with a spring or gas ram rifle. The PCP is capable of achieving a higher level of

A gun that exhibits recoil, even a phenomenal one like this Theoben Evolution gas ram, cannot compete with a PCP.

consistency than can be offered by a spring or gas ram and, although I enjoy shooting a spring gun – I find the challenge of controlling the recoil phase a stimulating one – I restrict my spring gun shooting to 30yd.

CARBINE BARREL OR LONG BARREL

There are a large number of carbine PCP rifles on the market today with very short barrels; these carbines are not all that manoeuvrable in the confined spaces you find in old farm buildings, grain lofts and the like. For such confined spaces special weapons, such as powerful pistols, are the only really manoeuvrable, fast fire weapons to use – carbine rifles are more a fashion statement than a practical innovation.

On a long-range hunting rifle you want a nice long barrel. You will not see a target rifle sporting a carbine barrel because target shooters understand the principle that a long barrel offers the projectile a smoother,

and therefore more stable, journey on its pathway down the bore. The projectile travelling down a long barrel will be subjected to a long, slow, very efficient push of air. A projectile coming down a tiny 9in barrel, however, will be followed by an extremely violent burst of air, because a short barrel demands the use of a large charge of air to produce the required velocity for stable flight. Whilst a weapon with a 9in barrel may produce a grouping sufficient for hunting purposes, a 19in barrel will produce an even tighter and more consistent grouping because a long barrel only requires a small charge of air in order to create the required velocity; thus it offers the pellet a much smoother push with less turbulence at the point of exit.

A longer barrel will also deliver a greater degree of rotation to the pellet. With a good air rifle one twist, that is a partial rotation of the pellet, will occur every ½in, it taking 17½in of travel to induce one complete rotation of the pellet. The more rotation of the pellet, the more stable it will be in flight, and

A long barrel like this 19in barrel on the Theoben Tactical offers a more efficient use of the air charge.

a long barrel obviously delivers more rotation than a short one.

This, at least, is the theory but, after conversations with a leading gun manufacturer, this theory was placed in doubt by the manufacturer suggesting that the length of the barrel had nothing to do with accuracy and was simply the selected choice of target shooters on a kind of placebo basis. The manufacturer's theory was that a longer barrel on a firearm aided the slow burning of the powder and therefore had no relevance to an air weapon. However, I remain convinced that a long barrel is the preferred option for long-range, accurate shooting, based entirely on the fact that a long barrel produces less turbulence behind the pellet as it exits the barrel.

If turbulence is not a contributing factor in the accuracy equation, why do target shooters fit strippers to the barrels of their rifles? The objective of the stripper is to strip away the air from behind the pellet, thus radically reducing the level of turbulence. A long barrel also makes very efficient use of air, requiring far less charge than a shorter barrel to stabilize a pellet in flight; you therefore get more shots per bottle charge with a long-barrelled rifle than you do with a short-barrelled one. This may not be of huge concern if operating with a 12ft/lb weapon in .20 calibre, but if you are using a .25 calibre rifle at 30 ft/lb it is of vital importance because the shot count of a long-barrelled Theoben in this format is roughly twenty shots per charge; using a shorter barrel would reduce that shot count.

MATCH GRADE TRIGGER

The next essential item on a long-range hunting air rifle is a match grade trigger of the very highest quality. A match grade trigger is one that is judged to be of sufficient quality that it could be fitted to a target rifle and used in shooting matches. Such a trigger will have a supremely smooth, two-stage action and offer a wide range of adjustment to the first and second stage of the trigger engagement, as well as providing some level of sear adjustment. We shall look at how to set a trigger correctly later on.

The trigger has to offer a wide range of adjustment because no two people have exactly the same finger movement or dexterity – what is right for one person is not necessarily right for another. However, the main objective in adjusting the trigger is to make the process of squeezing the trigger and disengaging the sear as light as possible. The less effort exerted by the trigger finger, in terms of pressure and movement, the less disturbance offered to the rifle and, the less a rifle moves, the more accurate it is. The ultimate trigger to have is a hair trigger, set so light that the weight of a single strand of hair laid on it will provide sufficient pressure to activate the sear. Such a trigger however, is something that you will have to progress towards as it takes extreme dexterity to handle. A lot of shooters say that hair triggers are dangerous, but that is not the case; they are only dangerous when in the hands of shooters who do not possess the level of skill required to manipulate them correctly.

REGULATORS

So far then on our list for a long-range hunter we have a long barrel and a match grade trigger, but what else is required? Do we need a regulator? A regulator is a device that measures the exact amount of air to be delivered to the breech. It measures out the same quantity of air every time a shot is made, so that every pellet will receive the same level of propellant force. This means that the trajectory taken by the pellets, although not identical, will be very similar indeed, thus ensuring a very high degree of consistency. Therefore each shot fired, because of the uniformity of the path taken from barrel to target, will hit almost the same mark, providing extremely tight groupings.

A PCP not fitted with a regulator will deliver charges of air that differ in measure from shot to shot and so, as the propelling force differs from one pellet to the next, the pellets will vary in trajectory and have differing strike points on the target. The ideal option for a long-range hunting air rifle is, therefore, to have one that is fitted with a regulator but, unfortunately, air rifles fitted with regulators are on the expensive side.

However, there is one air rifle not fitted with a regulator that delivers very reliable measures of air, with such small levels of differential that it offers a very respectable degree of consistency: that rifle is the Theoben Mk1. We shall look at this rifle more closely later in the chapter, but it is one of a very few unregulated guns that I consider capable of engaging live targets at 40yd. If your budget can stretch, it is infinitely preferable to go for a rifle with a regulator. A Theoben Mk1 will cost about £680, whereas a Theoben fitted with a regulator will cost between £830 and £940. If you do opt for a Mk1 then it can be upgraded and fitted with a regulator at the Theoben factory at a later date.

There are, apparently, large numbers of articles on the internet, telling the reader how to adjust the regulator on a Theoben, supposedly to increase the power output. If you come across such articles I would advise you to ignore them; the Theoben factory has gone to great lengths to test the regulators to find the optimum performance level to which they are set. If you tinker with your regulator you will, more than likely, end up injuring the efficiency of the weapon. There are items on a gun that should be adjusted, like the trigger and the stock, but the regulator should be left well alone and will then give years of trouble-free, efficient service.

MADE TO ORDER

A long-range hunting air rifle should be a custom-made weapon that has been put together with your specific needs taken into account. Nearly every air rifle on the market today will be purchased in its finished form, and there are no adjustments or alterations that can be made, other than to the trigger

*The DayState
Huntsman, a quality
British-made rifle.*

weight. But a few guns, like those in the Theoben range, can be made to order to suit the customer's exact needs: from the length and calibre of the barrel, to the configuration of the stock and the construction of the internals. In fact, a factory like Theoben can make any adjustments that you want, ensuring that you get the right gun for the job.

Buying a gun off the shelf is all well and good for most jobs, but you will always find that it has some weakness that niggles you. While such tiny niggles can be mastered when shooting at ranges out to 30yd, when it comes to tackling the long-range shot, the gun you are using has to be perfect, blending seamlessly with your body so that it is hard to tell where the shooter ends and the gun begins.

For this kind of gun you need to have something that was built for you by the best gun makers in the world and, for my money, that means a Theoben rifle. Theoben build my long-range hunting rifles and they are masterpieces of the gunsmiths' trade; although not cheap, they are the kind of air rifle capable of tackling long-range shots with ease.

Daystate is another British airgun manufacturer capable of building a gun to meet the customer's exact requirements. However, if you do opt for an off-the-shelf gun, then it can be taken to the required level for long-range work, by having a custom gun workshop perform their magic on it. Such workshops can create truly amazing weapons that can perform beyond your wildest dreams. Mass-produced, factory-made guns, which generally originate from foreign countries, may be affordable but they will not perform to the same high standard as a precision-made, British-built gun.

FULLY ADJUSTABLE STOCK

When it comes to the stock on a long-range hunting air rifle, the greater the degree of adjustment the stock offers the better; standard stocks, no matter how good they are, have been manufactured to meet the needs of the average person – who does not exist – so the standard stock is always a compromise. What is needed to achieve a bespoke fit is to a) have a stock made specifically for you which, although perfectly possible, is extremely expensive or b) have a stock that offers adjustment in the cheek piece and butt

The adjustable stock of the Theoben Rapid Tactical T1.

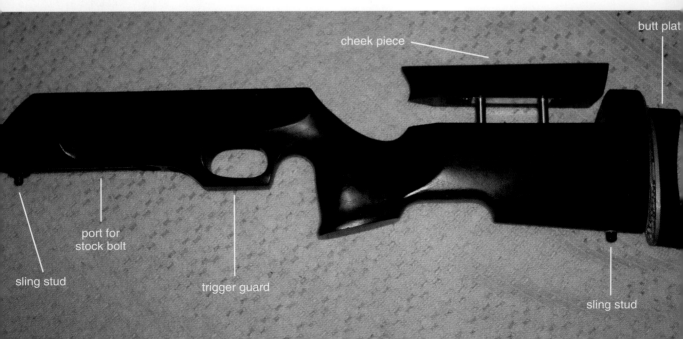

plate so that the stock can be set to conform precisely to the exact peculiarities of your body. There are only half a dozen hunting air rifles that have a fully adjustable stock.

It is astonishing that more airgun manufacturers do not offer a stock with multiple adjustments, therefore allowing it to become bespoke to the owner of the weapon. The better the join between gun and shooter, the more accurate the shots taken will be, which is why every target air rifle on the market has, as standard, a fully adjustable stock. Hunters who have traditionally used a standard, non-adjustable stock, who make the switch to a fully adjustable stock, soon discover a marked difference in the accuracy they are able to achieve.

As to the material used to make the stock, it really does not matter; fully adjustable stocks are at the high end of the market and so, whether they are made from a synthetic material or wood, they will be of the highest quality. On a wooden stock that means top quality walnut, which has a very tight grain and is one of the toughest woods in the world – it will last a lifetime if properly cared for.

CALIBRES

There are four calibres: .177 .20 .22 and .25. Each has its own distinct character, with perceptible advantages as well as disadvantages. As a hunter you need to weigh up the

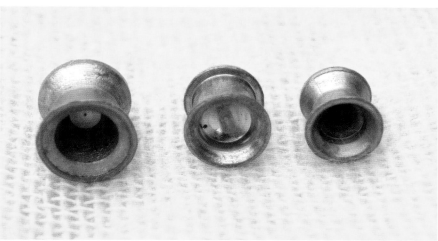

Pellets sized, left to right, .25, .22 and .20.

positives and negatives, to see which calibre presents the best profile for the kind of shooting that you will be engaging in. The main criteria are accuracy and power.

The current fashion is for accuracy, but I have always been a great advocate of power; I see very little point in delivering a pinpoint shot, exactly on target, if it does not have sufficient shock impact to create a sudden, fatal injury that will cause instant death. I have seen a .177 pellet delivered from an FAC-rated rifle to a rabbit's head, precisely where the pellet should be delivered, and yet watched the rabbit hop away. The pellet was deadly accurate, but it did not possess the kind of potent power needed to inflict a devastating, ragged wound tract that would have caused fatal damage to the blood vessels. The nature of the wound the .177 pellet created was more surgical in nature; the pellet, unwilling to dump its energy, travelled right through the rabbit's head, leaving a smooth wound tract which, though fatal, caused a slow and inhumane death, rather than an instant dispatch.

I am therefore a firm believer in power: the transfer of energy from the pellet to the quarry at the point of impact. In order to achieve this you need a big pellet – the bigger the better – which is why my favourite calibre is .25. To use this substantial pellet at ranges of 40yd and beyond, you will need to have a rifle with a power output rating beyond 12ft/lb. This places the air rifle in the firearms category and thus you will require a firearms certificate. The level of power you will require to deploy a .25 rifle on targets at 40yd and beyond is in the range 16ft/lb to 30ft/lb.

The figures are based on discussions with Theoben's top gun engineer, who told me that experiments at the factory with the .25 calibre have revealed that the most efficient power setting is in the stated range. With this kind of power setting the trajectory of the .25 pellet flattens, so the arch from the muzzle to the target becomes markedly less steep. The flatter the trajectory, the more accurate the weapon, for the simple reason that the line of sight and the path of the projectile

are closer together, making it easier to align the two. The flat trajectory of the .177 pellet makes it extremely accurate and explains why so many air gun hunters have decided to utilize it on live quarry. However, I do not consider the .177 to provide sufficient trauma on impact for efficient, clean kills. There is a famous American elk hunter who, when asked his opinion, always says power is more important than velocity and, as a pest controller, I totally agree with him.

The .177 pellet may offer velocity and a flat trajectory, but it does not provide sufficient power at the strike point. However, when you increase the power rating of the .25 to the level of 16ft/lb to 30ft/lb, you have a weapon that offers a flat trajectory, combined with a phenomenal degree of impact, taking the airgun to a whole new level of operation and bringing live targets at 50 and even 60yd into play. If you have a firearms certificate, which you need in order to own an air rifle operating above 12ft/lb, why bother with an air rifle at all, why not just go for a .22 bullet rifle and take your target engagement range up to 100yd? With the air rifle in .25, operating at 30ft/lb, even if a body shot is taken, it causes a minimal amount of damage to the meat of the animal, whereas a bullet, delivered to the body of a rabbit at 1000ft/lb, smashes it to pieces, making the air rifle the preferred option for the gathering of meat.

The .25 pellet, working at 12ft/lb, is operating at the very lowest end of its thrust requirements; there is just enough propulsive force at this power setting to stabilize the pellet in flight. When the pellet goes past 30yd, it is unable to sustain sufficient rotation to maintain a stable flight path and, although it still retains sufficient strike force in this unstable state to impart significant damage, it is not stable enough to allow for accurate placement. Over 30yd a .25 pellet, fired from the very best air rifle in the world set at 12ft/lb will, when aimed at a mark in the centre of an A3 sheet of paper, completely miss the mark, the pellets striking the sheet one at the top, another at the bottom, with no two pellets striking the same mark. The resulting grouping could be anywhere between 1 and 2ft which, of course, makes the .25 rifle in 12ft/lb completely unviable for long-range shooting at live targets.

If you select .25 as your calibre of choice for long-range, advanced hunting, you will have to apply for a firearms certificate, which is not difficult. Converting an existing 12ft/lb .25 rifle, such as the Theoben Tactical, into a 16ft/lb to 30ft/lb rifle, only requires a slight adjustment to the level of tension on the hammer spring and some adjustment to the regulator. Although this work is very easy to carry out, you will have to have it performed by a registered gunsmith as the weapon, once the modifications have been made, will have to be placed on the firearms register, which has to be done by a registered gunsmith.

If you wish to take the power setting of your rifle even higher, up to 40ft/lb, then you would, along with the modifications already mentioned, need to have the regulator replaced and have the barrel port enlarged. The barrel port is the opening in the base of the barrel through which air enters behind the pellet. A rifle like the Theoben Tactical, set at 40ft/lb, will offer roughly twenty shots per charge, which is more than sufficient for a day's rabbit hunting – the advanced airgun hunter will rarely miss and ninety-nine per cent of all shots will achieve a one-shot kill.

In my opinion, the .25 calibre is perfect for the advanced airgun hunter. It is the most efficient of all the projectiles at killing quarry, due to its size and the fact that the slower travelling pellet is easier to destabilize than pellets with a greater velocity; thus it will dump its energy at, or shortly after, the point of impact, with the effect of creating a devastating wound tract, far in excess of anything that the other calibre pellets can make, resulting in fatal trauma and a clean kill.

The .25 pellet is also much more willing to deform on impact than the other calibre pellets, this means that over-penetration of the target is considerably less likely to

The .25 pellet head deforms significantly on impact.

occur, even when using a firearms-rated rifle. Deformed pellets also do not maintain a straight path through the vital organs of the target quarry, but deviate offline, spreading the trauma effect over a much larger area than can be achieved by pellets from the other calibres. The historical prejudice toward the .25 calibre has always been against its accuracy. The theory that is universally accepted, and is rarely challenged, being that the .25 rifle is an inaccurate weapon, only capable of delivering very short-range shots. This is most certainly not the case, as a modern .25 PCP manufactured by Theoben is capable of putting together groupings of 15mm or less, which means that the grouping will fit beneath a five pence piece.

This kind of accuracy is what you would expect to achieve with a match target rifle, so the argument that the .25 is inaccurate is completely flawed. However, the 12ft/lb .25 rifle is not a long-range weapon, although it is not restricted to the 20yd range generally quoted as the maximum range of a non-FAC .25. A non-FAC .25 will, in fact, operate out

A chronograph.

to 30yd, which is the maximum range at which all air rifles should be operated, other than for a handful of very special precision rifles. Firing the Theoben Rapid in .25 over a chronograph reveals a variance of just 7fps (feet per second); with the rifle set at 16ft/lb the variance goes down to 5. Variance is calculated by carrying out a string of shots over a chronograph: the string being between fifteen and thirty shots. The chronograph will measure the velocity of these shots in fps, you record them all on a sheet of paper, deduct the lowest velocity from the highest velocity recorded, and the figure you get is your rifle's variance. The lower the variance, the more consistent the weapon and, therefore, the more accurate.

Consistency – the uniform delivery of pellets from the barrel in the same shape and with the same propulsive force behind them – is the key to accuracy. Consistency is measured by variance – the lower the variance figure, the higher the consistency – thus the greater the potential for accuracy. A variance of seven to ten is extremely good, a variance of four to six is exceptional, and a variance above fifteen in a precision-made weapon is a cause for concern. We shall be looking at variance again later, when we come to the subject of selecting the correct ammunition for the long-range shooter.

Some readers will be concerned with pest control operations, relating to feral pigeons and starlings (in Scotland only, where starlings are allowed to be destroyed under a general license issued by the ministry). Such operations generally take place inside large farm buildings and the .25 calibre set at 30 to 40ft/lb offers too much power for the task for two reasons. Firstly, when carrying out pest control work you are looking at taking large numbers of birds – it could be anything from 50 to 100 or even more – and so you want a weapon with a significant shot count per bottle charge. This is not something offered by a .25 delivering in excess of 30ft/lb, the best shot count you could hope for being roughly thirty or so shots per bottle charge. This means making numerous visits to your vehicle to recharge, which is time-consuming and inconvenient, especially if you are working from a hide, so you would be much better served by a .25 calibre weapon with a power setting of 16 to18ft/lb.

This slight increase on the legal limit will take the power setting up to a level where it is able to deliver a pellet out to a range of 40 to 45yd, turning the rifle into a long-range hunter, whilst keeping the shot count nice and high. The Theoben rifle offers roughly 100 to 150 shots per bottle charge when set at 16 to 18ft/lb of power output. To take the rifle up to such a power setting would also not cost too much; all that is required is an adjustment to the tension level of the hammer spring, no new parts or re-machining are necessary, although the adjustment will still have to be carried out by a gunsmith, who will place the weapon on the firearms register once the work is completed and you will, of course, need a firearms certificate as the rifle will become a class one firearm.

The other reason you do not want 30 to 40ft/lb of power output when performing pest control operations inside farm buildings, is because the killing range of such a pellet propelled by such a force is 70 to 90yd. This means that if you do miss your target, you have a very powerful projectile zipping around inside an enclosed space, that possesses more than enough power to shoot a hole in the roof; if it should happen to ricochet off a steel girder on which feral pigeons and starlings love to perch, then you had better hope the pellet does not strike you when it has that kind of power behind it. A rifle knocking out 30 to 40ft/lb of power is more than capable of killing a human being if the pellet hits the right place, so this is not the kind of power output to be using inside farm buildings or around farmyards.

I have spent some time looking at the .25 calibre, which I consider to be the ultimate airgun calibre for the serious hunter and pest controller, however I fully understand that many people are not willing to go to the lengths required to acquire a firearms certificate. Although the acquisition of a firearms certificate is quite straightforward, for those who do not wish to go down that route, we need to decide which calibre is best suited to the needs of the long-range, advanced airgun hunter, operating within the constraints of the 12ft/lb limit.

Airgun hunters today fall staunchly into one of two categories: the .177 camp, and the .22 camp, and never the twain shall meet. The .177 camp argue with great vigour that the .177 is the ultimate calibre because of its flat trajectory, which facilitates extreme accuracy, while the .22 camp argue with equal vigour that the .22 is the ultimate calibre because it offers a heavy degree of impact. One camp favours velocity, the other power; but there is a third option, which offers a flat trajectory and significant impact, as well as combining the best qualities of the .177 with those of the .22.

That option is the .20, which, astonishingly, is one that only a handful of the most knowledgeable airgunners take. It is amazing how many airgun hunters do not even know that this calibre exists, mainly because there are only a handful of .20 calibre rifles available. I am aware of only one manufacturer that produces PCP weapons in this unique and very effective calibre, and that manufacturer is Theoben, who hold this calibre in

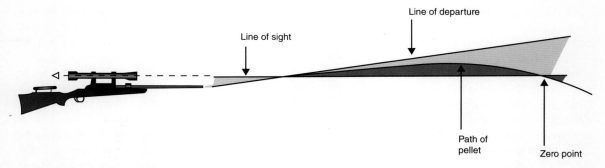

Line of sight

Line of departure

Path of pellet

Zero point

The line of sight in relation to pellet trajectory.

very high regard due to its performance in the hunting field. The .20 is the perfect long-range hunting pellet, because it offers a nice flat trajectory, allowing for easy alignment between the line of sight and pellet arc.

The .20 really is a very accurate pellet capable, when fired from a quality gun like the Theoben Mk1, of putting together a 15mm grouping at 40yd. Although the .177 camp would argue that their calibre is able to do the same, they cannot argue that it is able to deliver a significant level of impact because the .177 is actually offering the very minimum level of impact required in the hunting field. The .20 pellet not only puts together a tight grouping, but it also carries some real sting on impact, smashing into the quarry with far more force than the puny .177 can muster. The dictionary definition for puny is inferior in size, strength and power and that just about sums up the .177. You may think that I have no regard for the .177 but you would be wrong; I consider it to be a phenomenally accurate calibre, however, I simply do not consider the field of hunting to be the correct utilization for this calibre.

Although I agree with the .22 camp that the .22 is most definitely a hunting calibre, I do not believe it is the most suitable for long-range shooting, because it cannot match the trajectory of the .20 and therefore cannot match it for accuracy. The .20 does not have the same amount of strike power as the .22, although it is not that far off. The .20 calibre

combines the best qualities of the .177 with those of the .22 and then throws into the pot some qualities of its own, to make it an incredibly stable pellet in flight.

I am located on the north-east coast of Scotland, in an area that is officially recognized as one of the windiest spots in Europe, so you can imagine how strong the winds are around here, making it the ideal place to test a pellet's stability in windy conditions. I can assert, with confidence, that the .20 is the most stable, having deployed this calibre with great success in gale-force winds. The pellets fired from a Theoben held true to their course, with very little compensation for wind needing to be made. I have included a photograph of a tarpaulin that was lashed down securely with strong rope, being blown about by the kind of winds I regularly hunt in, to give you a visual indication of the kind of winds that the .20 can cope with easily.

In the .20 we see a flat trajectory, significant strike power, and an amazing level of stability in flight for such a small projectile, all of which adds up to the perfect equation for a long-range hunting pellet. The question must therefore be asked, why would anyone choose to select any other calibre for a long-range shot where 12ft/lb is the power output being used? All of the PCP rifles in the Theoben range can be offered in .20 calibre and most of the top pellet manufactures have a .20 pellet in their range, some of which are exceptionally good.

The effect of the wind in the north-east of Scotland.

PRESSURE GAUGES

A pressure gauge tells you how much air there is remaining in the rifle's air reservoir and, though such gauges are not essential, they are extremely useful as regards long range shooting. In order to carry out a humane, long range shot successfully, you have to be confident that there is sufficient air in the reservoir to take the pellet to the target with full power behind it. The Theoben rifles have an incredible shot capacity of 400 shots per charge and it is quite easy to lose count of how many shots you have fired. You have to be disciplined about replenishing the air reservoir, before or after each hunting expedition, which many hunters fail to do. Instead they prefer to grab their rifle in the excitement of the moment, trusting that they have got sufficient air left in the reservoir to do the job,

and then find themselves in a position where there is insufficient air in the reservoir to deliver a fatal shot at range.

Having a small pressure gauge fitted to your rifle ensures that this does not happen, as once glance at these easily read gauges gives you an instant report on the status of your air reserves. If you are shooting a firearms-rated .25 Theoben rifle, capable of smashing out 30ft/lb, you will only have a shot capacity of twenty shots per buddy bottle fill and, in the heat of the hunt, it is all too easy to lose track of your shot count; a pressure gauge is therefore the only sure way to keep an accurate check on your air reserves with an FAC-rated weapon.

Keeping track of your shot count is much more important with the .25 FAC-rated rifle because, once you hit shot number twenty, there is no longer sufficient air left in the buddy bottle to carry another pellet out to a long-range target, with sufficient force to guarantee a clean kill. Therefore, from a humane point of view – which should be the cornerstone of your hunting ethics – it is vital to have a method of monitoring the level of air present in the reservoir. All Theoben rifles can be fitted with a pressure status gauge when you purchase them. If you have an older Theoben rifle that is not fitted with a pressure status gauge, then you can fit one yourself using the DIY kit supplied by Theoben or, if you do not feel up to the task, it can be done at the Theoben factory for you.

SILENCERS

Most airgun hunters have a silencer fitted to their rifle, simply as a means of making the weapon a little bit quieter when it discharges. This is a useful feature, as firing a silenced weapon does not alert the target quarry to your presence; thus, if there are numerous target animals in range you do not scare them all off when you dispatch one. This allows you to take several animals, rather than the single animal you would get if using a weapon that produced more noise on discharge.

But there is another feature of the silencer that most shooters completely overlook, which has a particular value to the long-range hunter. This feature is the ability to strip away air from behind the speeding pellet, so that there is less turbulence behind the pellet when it exits the silencer. The theory being that the less turbulence behind the pellet at the point of exit, the truer and more stable its flight from barrel to target. Most target shooters have a device called a stripper fitted to the muzzle of their rifles and, although these devices do not reduce the muzzle blast at all, in fact they may make it even louder, they do draw away a substantial amount of the air from behind the pellet.

The long series vortex silencer from Theoben.

Not a single quality target rifle is produced today without one of these devices being fitted as standard, so the target fraternity is obviously convinced that the removal of turbulence from behind the exiting pellet is an essential requirement for the accurate and consistent placement of pellets upon the target. I am convinced that this is the case, but the hunter cannot use a stripper due to the noise it creates. However, we can use the next best thing, which is a long silencer, such as the long series vortex silencer manufactured by Theoben, which is ideally suited to the job of removing turbulence. So a long silencer is an essential requirement that must be present on a rifle intended for engaging long-range, live targets.

THE PERFECT LONG-RANGE HUNTING RIFLE

Now that we have meticulously gone through the essential attributes that the long-range hunting air rifle must possess, let me introduce you to the perfect example of a long-range hunter. In my opinion the best hunting rifle to be found anywhere in the world today is the Theoben Tactical with a Rapid 7 action; the weapon being set up in .25 calibre for FAC holders or in .20 calibre for those preferring the 12ft/lb format. This is the rifle that I use and I will take you on a journey around this gun from the muzzle to the butt, showing you how to set up this rifle for long-range shooting, how to keep it clean and lubricated, how to monitor its power output and how to mount a scope upon it. Target shooters are always tinkering with their weapons, looking for tiny little adjustments that could improve accuracy, even if the improvement is only a tiny hundredth of a millimetre. The advanced airgun hunter, like the serious target shooter, must have the skill to make tiny adjustments to the weapon they are using, in order to get the optimum performance out of it. So, let us begin with the first part of the weapon that comes into contact with the shooter's body: the stock.

SETTING UP THE STOCK

An adjustable stock offers two areas of adjustment: these are to the position of the butt plate and the position of the cheek piece. The adjustment in the butt plate is to allow the plate to fit neatly into the shoulder pocket that occurs where the chest muscle and the shoulder muscle, known as the deltoid, meet. The curve on the end of the butt plate is designed to follow the natural descending curve of this pocket, which of course varies in dimensions from one person to the next, which is why movement in the butt plate is required in order to achieve the best fitting of the butt plate to the shoulder pocket.

To facilitate the correct adjustment of a moveable butt plate, loosen the single screw in the back of the plate so that the plate can move up and down its guide rail. Do not over-loosen the screw; it is far better to have the plate moving fairly stiffly rather than having it moving with no resistance, as a completely free-moving plate is difficult to set in the desired position. Set the plate at what you think is the correct location, then raise the weapon to the shoulder, looking through the scope at a mark to see if the adjustment is correct. The aim is to have the butt plate as deeply embedded in the shoulder pocket as it can possibly be, with complete contact occurring between the shooter's body and the butt plate.

As the main meeting place between shooter and rifle, this union needs to be as seamless as possible, so take time to get the positioning just right. Try a variety of different positions to see which is the most comfortable; you will never successfully engage long-range targets if you feel uncomfortable.

I personally like my butt plate set very low so that the plate wraps round into the armpit, but many shooters would find this uncomfortable – it all depends on the muscle culture that the shooter possesses in the area of the shoulder pocket. I do a lot of weight training so my chest muscles are quite well developed and I find that if the butt plate is set too high the chest muscle tends to push the rifle away from the body; I therefore set my butt plate lower, which overcomes this slight difficulty. Look carefully at the physical construction of your shoulder pocket to decide the best location for the butt plate, and do not set up your butt plate like someone else, even if they are an exceptional shot, because you are different to that person and so your requirements are different.

If the butt plate is set too high you will also notice a gap between the top of the butt plate and the body, which is undesirable: the greater the contact between the body and the butt plate, the better the support platform you provide. Once you have settled on the correct site for the butt plate, lock it in place by tightening the screw in the back of the plate. You have set the plate in the standing position, so you should now take up the kneeling and the prone positions to see if the butt plate's position is also comfortable in these shooting positions: the change in position means the muscles move, thus changing the shape of the shoulder pocket and the position of the head.

Target shooters have classes that are at set ranges in a specified position, for example 10m standing, so they can set up the entire rifle to accommodate a single firing position. However, we as hunters must set up the rifle in a slightly compromised fashion so that it suits all the shooting positions that we have to take. It is no good having the butt plate in the perfect location for the standing position if it does not work well in the prone position; you need to compromise slightly and adjust the site of the butt plate so that it matches both positions. If, however, you know that the shooting you are going to be doing on a specific outing is only going to require the use of one position, then you could set up the butt plate for that position. If you have never used a rifle with an adjustable, bespoke, butt plate, set to the contours of your shoulder pocket before, you will be amazed how much difference it makes to the fit of the gun from a comfort and accuracy point of view.

Now that you have set the butt plate to its optimum location for your needs, it is time to turn your attention to the setting of the cheek piece. The reason that you move the cheek piece is to achieve perfect alignment between the eye of the shooter and the exit pupil of the scope. Light entering the objective lens of a scope is funnelled along the tube to a number of concave and convex

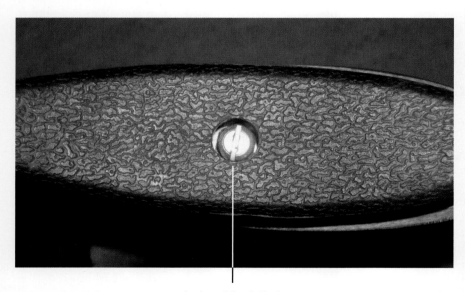

slacken this slotted
screw slightly to facilitate
movement in the butt plate

*Setting the position
of the butt plate.*

*1 Loosen the locking
screw in the back of
the plate.*

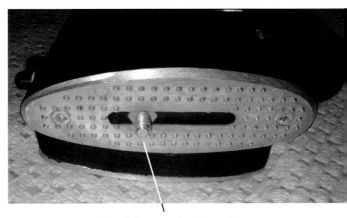

the sliding mechanism of
the movable butt plate

ABOVE: *2 Move the plate along the guide rail to the desired location.*

LEFT: *3 Test the fit of the butt plate to the shoulder pocket.*

BELOW: *4 Tighten the locking screw when the optimum union between the plate and shoulder is achieved.*

ote the full contact between
e shoulder pocket and the
butt plate

lenses that invert and right the image as it travels down the tube. The light enters the very centre of these lenses, through an area known as the exit pupil, which you can see for yourself if you hold up a scope at arm's length and look through the ocular lens. The circle that you will see in the centre of the lens is the exit pupil and, in order to use a scope correctly, the centre of your eye needs to be lined up directly behind the exit pupil. This means keeping the shooter's head erect and not bent over the comb, as any leaning of the head will bring about a position where the shooter is not looking through the centre of the exit pupil or using the centre of their eye; both of these factors will compromise the image that the shooter will receive.

Poor head placement will lead to eye-strain, inconsistent images, poor accuracy, poor range finding and poor clarity of the image viewed. Therefore, it is easy to see that the correct locating of the head against the cheek piece, which in turn leads to the alignment of the exit pupil and the centre of the eye, is not merely desirable but an essential element of accurate shooting. A shooter may get away with poor head placement when engaging targets at 30yd or less, but when the range is extended to the very limits of the rifle's capabilities (40 to 45yd for 12ft/lb and 50 to 60yd for FAC 30ft/lb), then fractions of a millimetre matter and, consequently, the perfect placement of the head and alignment of scope and eye is of paramount importance to facilitate such a demanding degree of accuracy.

At such ranges, poor head placement will lead to missed shots, or worse, non-fatal injuries, which is the most catastrophic thing that you can do, causing extreme suffering to a wild animal. No target shooter would ever consider using a weapon that did not have an adjustable cheek piece; extreme accuracy with a rifle is deemed to be impossible to achieve without using a stock that can be set to bring about bespoke eye alignment with the exit pupil.

As hunters, we can learn a lesson here from the target shooters and follow their lead by using an adjustable cheek piece on hunting rifles to improve the level of achievable accuracy. The cheek piece on the Theoben Tactical hunting rifle is adjustable in two different planes: the vertical and the lateral. You will notice that stocks curve slightly away from the cheek; this is not to make the stock look good but to allow the head to move behind the scope. If the stock were a square piece of wood, your eye would not be able to get behind the scope unless you bent your head, which is an incorrect placement.

The sloping away of the stock however, may be a little too acute, or not sufficiently deep to suit the contours of your cheek structure, for the simple reason that we all have different-shaped faces. And this is why Theoben have built lateral movement into the check piece, not as much as you would see in a target rifle, but sufficient to allow the hunter to position their eye directly behind the scope.

This lateral movement of several millimetres is accessed by first, fully loosening the cheek piece screw, located on the right hand side of the stock, which will allow you to slide out the cheek piece. Next turn the cheek piece upside down and you will see a plate containing the two extension rods that facilitate vertical movement. At either end of this plate there is located a small screw. If you slightly loosen these screws you will discover that the plate has a small amount of lateral movement. Move the plate to the required position, then tighten the screws and reassemble. If the degree of adjustment is not sufficient to get your eye directly behind the scope, then undo the screws once more and remove the plate completely, so that you can run a wood file along the edge of the recess into which the plate fits. You will also have to enlarge the holes in the plate using a small drill. If you do make this modification, remember that the adjustments you make should be very small, no more than a couple of millimetres, as this is all that is required to get the eye into the desired position.

Setting the cheek piece

1 Loosen the locking screw.

slacken this hex headed screw
to release the cheek piece

2 Remove the cheek piece.

off side view of the stock

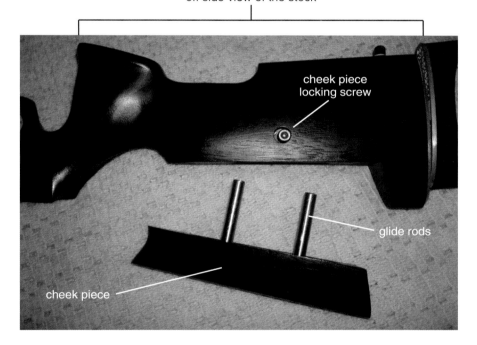

cheek piece
locking screw

glide rods

cheek piece

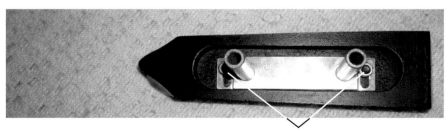

3 Turn the cheek piece upside down.

loosen these nuts to facilitate lateral adjustment
in the position of the cheek piece

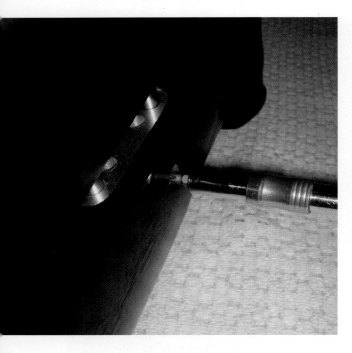

4 Replace the cheek piece and tighten the locking screw slightly, allowing just sufficient slack for movement of the cheek piece up and down.

BELOW: 5 Move the cheek piece up and down to acquire the correct setting, that being the top of the cheek piece aligned with the base of the cheekbone.

The head needs to be kept in the upright position so that the centre of the eye, rather than the side, is used and so the cheek piece needs to be set at a height that encourages the head to stay erect, directly behind the scope. Again, you need to have adjustment in the cheek piece because people have different-shaped faces; therefore someone with a long neck and thin face is going to have the cheek piece set in a different location to the person with a short neck and rounded face.

If you set the cheek piece too high it will push the cheek away from the required line of alignment behind the scope, whilst if you set it too low it will encourage the head to lean over the cheek piece, which will again destroy the desired alignment. The correct location is to have the top of the cheek piece set at a height where, with the rifle shouldered, it lines up with the base of the cheekbone. In this position the cheek should assume full and firm contact with the cheek piece.

To facilitate vertical movement in the cheek piece on the Theoben Tactical precision hunting rifle, loosen the cheek piece locking screw, located on the right hand side of the stock, which will allow you to move the cheek piece to the required height. You can test this by shouldering the rifle and noting the location of the top of the cheek piece against the cheekbone. Once the correct height is selected, retighten the locking screw and the stock is then fully bespoke, set to the individual characteristics of your face.

There is one last point to be made about the stock; left-handed shooters will say that you will never achieve the required standard of accuracy for long-range, live target engagement with a weapon mounted in a right-handed stock. Left-handed stocks do exist, and are essential for the left-handed shooter in order for them to achieve the correct alignment between the eye and the scope. All you have to do to have a Theoben precision hunting rifle mounted in a left-handed stock, is contact the Theoben factory and they will arrange one for you.

SETTING THE TRIGGER

[See the labelled photograph later in this chapter for the layout of the trigger.]

In order to understand how to set up the trigger, you must also understand the principles of a trigger control method called the 'Smooth Action' method, which is used by snipers in the US military and is the technique taught to Navy Seals, who are among the world's very finest precision shots. The principal of the smooth pull is simple, and is applied once the cross hairs have been lined up with the kill zone of the target quarry. If you are satisfied that the quarry is going to maintain its position for the several seconds it will take to depress the trigger, you move your finger smoothly down from its waiting position on the stock and place it on the trigger blade, where it takes up the free play on the trigger, known as the first stage.

Then comes a tiny pause whilst you perfect the aim, aligning the cross hairs with pinpoint precision on the kill zone and, as the cross hairs come into perfect alignment, a breath pause is applied and the remaining trigger pull, known as the second stage, is engaged, releasing the hammer that brings about the release of a charge of air.

In order to carry out this kind of trigger control, the first stage of the trigger's engagement needs to present sufficient pressure to define it from the second stage, and sufficient pressure for the finger to read its movement. If the first stage were set so light that a fly landing on it would fully engage it, then the shooter in the field, required to pause between first and second stage engagement, would be forgiven for moving right through the first stage and gliding into the second stage, all in the one action. This is fine when shooting at paper targets that do not move, but when shooting at live prey, such as rabbits that are prone to move whilst you are trying to deliver your shot, the steady, methodical approach of the smooth action method should used.

However, once the aim is perfected you do not want there do be any delay whatsoever.

You want the second stage to engage as quickly and as smoothly as possible; this means having it set as light as possible in the hair pin trigger mode, requiring no more than the weight of a single hair to engage it and requiring the merest movement of the trigger finger to send the pellet spinning down the barrel.

For the smooth action method of trigger control to work, you need to have the first stage moderately set, and the second stage set as light as you can possibly cope with. The Theoben trigger unit offers adjustment to the setting of the sear; this you should leave alone as the factory setting is perfect for the requirements of the long-range hunter. The first stage of the trigger pull on this trigger is already set to a moderate level, with sufficient slack and pressure upon full engagement for the first stage to be well read by the trigger finger. This ensures that the finger does not ride right through it into the second stage so, on this trigger unit, the first stage setting should be left as it is.

If you are using another make of rifle and the first stage is set a little on the heavy side, then adjust it onto a moderate setting. Now comes the second stage and, before you make any adjustment, take a piece of paper and a pencil and make a note of every turn made to the adjustment screw. Then, if you mess the whole thing up, all you have to do to get back to the factory setting to have another go is to count up the number of turns made to the adjustment screw and reapply them. To make the second stage lighter, turn the second stage adjustment screw out, making only one half turn at a time, then try the trigger. Keep making adjustments until the trigger is as light as you can handle and keep a record of how many half turns you applied in order to reach a setting that is bespoke to your trigger control ability, so that should you ever need to return to the factory setting it is easily done.

KEEPING YOUR PRECISION RIFLE CLEAN

Whenever carrying out maintenance procedures on your rifle, first make it safe and remove the air bottle.

Many hunters do nothing or very little in the way of cleaning their weapon, whereas the target shooter is fastidious to the point of obsession; so which of these is right? Which approach best facilitates the accurate placement of shots at long range?

Because much of my initial weapons training was done with firearms in the military, I tend to stand firmly in the camp of cleaning a weapon till it gleams like a new pin; by that I do not just mean polishing what can be seen, but getting inside the weapon to clean the barrel and lubricate the trigger. Lubrication, believe it or not, has a direct correlation with the level of accuracy that you will be able to achieve, for the simple reason that a well-lubricated component, like the trigger, will move smoothly as it was intended to do, whereas a dry trigger will have a stiffer action. This causes a greater degree of disturbance to be transmitted from the shooter to the gun because of the increased level of mechanical effort required to depress the trigger. The difference in the pressure required to depress a well-lubricated trigger, and that required to depress a dry trigger may be minimal, but when it comes to placing pellets with pinpoint accuracy at long range then even minuscule differences have a noticeable effect.

Correct trigger lubrication is therefore essential, for the simple reason that oils and greases dry out over a period of time due to exposure to the elements and the movement of working parts. A lot of hunters will argue that cleaning the barrel is not necessary because the barrel has to be leaded, meaning it must have a lining of pellet lead in order to achieve its full potential as regards accuracy. This may well be the case, but target shooters clean their barrels, and then re-lead them by sending a number of shots down the barrel. A practical clean is all that is required; however, an oiled barrel patch on a pull through is not going to remove all the lead from a barrel, just the dirt and excess lead particles that could cause a problem.

In order to achieve total lead removal you would need to resort to the use of brass brushes and bore solvents, which are not the kind of items that you want to be putting into your rifle's barrel unless you intend to damage it. Just a few passes with a cleaning rod down the barrel of an air rifle can damage the choke, destroying the barrel's accuracy. Bore solvents are designed to remove the kind of stubborn deposits left behind deep in the barrel of a firearm, caused by the burning effect when the cartridge is ignited, so are not designed for air rifle barrels.

Airgun hunters use their rifles in agricultural areas where the weapon is going to get wet and dirty. I live in an agricultural area where potatoes and barley are grown; whenever a tractor works on the fields around my property, if my car is not parked in the garage a cloud of dust descends upon it, with billions of tiny particles of grit forming a blanket that is thick enough to write your name in.

The point I am trying to make is that, when out shooting in an agricultural area, those tiny particles of grit will get inside the barrel of the rifle and a build-up of dirt or lead particles in the choke area of the barrel can have a serious effect on the rifle's zero, shifting the point of impact. At 30yd the shift will be considered small and insignificant and can be lived with, but when operating at the limit of the rifle's killing range, such tiny shifts can mean the difference between a clean kill and a wounding, as the further away from the barrel the pellet gets, the greater the shift becomes.

The countryside is a dirty place and any mechanical device employed in the countryside is going to get dirty and, in order to keep it functioning, it needs to be cleaned. A dirty barrel may well perform adequately out to 30yd, but for the kind of pinpoint accuracy we are looking for as an advanced airgun hunter, engaging targets at long range, a dirty barrel will have a negative effect on accuracy and therefore the barrel of your rifle must be cleaned after every outing.

Another prime reason why the barrel of your rifle has to be cleaned is to protect it from the build-up of corrosion by the removal of moisture. Moisture in the atmosphere is the catalyst that sets off the corrosion process, which is why its removal is so important. Any rifle that has been out on a cold winter's day is going to be exposed to atmospheric moisture, both externally and internally, so the barrel should be cleaned as soon as practically possible after each hunt. Some may argue that the lead lining of the barrel is sufficient protection from moisture, but for that to be true, every single part of the barrel would have to have an even coating of lead, no part of the barrel being left bare, which is not the case. Even the slightest microscopic scratch would open up the lead skin to reveal the steel barrel beneath. Not all hunters actually use lead pellets any more, as there are plenty of alloy alternatives on the market today, which are extremely good, and, of course, such pellets do not leave behind a protective coating.

In order to be protected from corrosion, a barrel needs to have the moisture removed from it and oil applied on a regular basis. Every other form of shooting recognizes this fact and it is only the airgun world that believes a neglected barrel will perform perfectly and never succumb to corrosion. I should qualify this statement by saying that it is only the hunting section of the airgun world that holds such a belief; the target section most certainly does not believe that a dirty barrel is a precision barrel.

To clean the barrel of the Theoben Tactical precision hunting rifle you will need to remove the barrel to do a proper job, which is a very simple operation, requiring nothing more complex than a few Allen keys. The first step in this operation is the removal of the scope. I can hear some shooters sighing with disbelief. I know that your scope is zeroed in and that when you remove it from the rifle it will remove your zeroing. When the scope is remounted the zeroing process will have to be carried out again, but that should not be a problem for an advanced airgun hunter; the removal and re-zeroing of a scope should be something that you take in your stride, being able to re-zero your weapon in a matter of minutes.

The other point is that you should never engage in any long-range hunting expedition before checking the zero of your scope, as there is no guarantee that the scope is still zeroed correctly. There is a possibility, even though it is a small one when talking about a quality scope, that since you last used the rifle the scope has lost its zero. This is why snipers and law enforcement marksmen check the zero of their scope every time they use their weapon with a device called a collimator. The reason that these professional marksmen are so punctilious is that they have to be sure that the first shot they take with their weapon is going to kill a dangerous criminal or enemy – any mistake in zero could mean the loss of innocent lives.

As a hunter with a moral code, based on the humane killing of the target quarry with the first shot, we are obliged to take the same approach as a professional marksman; if we do not there is always the possibility that one day the first shot we make with the rifle will wound, because the scope's zero has shifted. Removing the scope should not present any problem whatsoever, and it is possible if you use a Weaver mounting system to remove the scope, then put it back in exactly the same place that you took it from.

It is a mystery to me why airgun hunters do not use the Weaver mounting system when it is so widely used in other areas of shooting, both hunting and tactical. All of the rifles in the Theoben range can be fitted with a Weaver rail and it makes life so much easier; I shall come back to the Weaver mounting system a little later in the chapter on scopes. So, when removing the barrel from the Theoben Tactical precision hunting rifle, if you are using a Weaver mounting system, you will simply need to loosen the base of the scope mounts, and the scope with the mount rings still fixed to it will lift off.

Make a mental note as you remove the scope as to the location of the mounts on the Weaver rail; this is easily done by counting the notches from the rear of the Weaver mount, to the location of the rear scope mount. The next step is to remove the Weaver rail, which is achieved by the removal of two screws.

If you use a Weaver system the scope can be removed with the mounting rings still on it.

Place the rail and the screws into a clean container so that nothing gets lost. If you look at the front portion of the block you will notice above the barrel, where it fits into the block, a very small locating screw, its job being to align the barrel with the block. Remove this screw with a slotted screwdriver and place it safely to one side.

Remove the Weaver rail by removing the screw indicated.

these two hex-headed screws secure the weaver rail to the block

Place all parts removed in a safe container to prevent loss or damage.

If you now look at the block from the side, you will see a recessed screw head, located just slightly higher than the barrel. It does not matter which side of the block you look at, as there is a screw on both sides. These screws hold the barrel clamp together, which is responsible for keeping the barrel securely in place. A lot of PCP rifles just have a single small screw holding the barrel in place, which is why they often come loose, but the clamp used on the Theoben range of PCPs never comes loose. Put an Allen key in both screw heads and turn one, which will loosen the clamp. Keep loosening the screw until you can remove it and the clamp from the block.

The barrel locating screw.

front of block

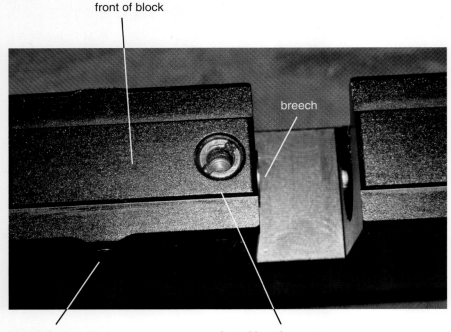

breech

barrel clamp screw

barrel locating screw

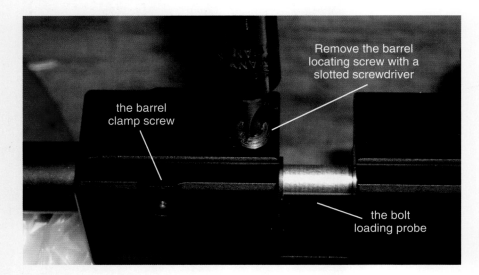

Remove the barrel locating screw with a slotted screwdriver

the barrel clamp screw

the bolt loading probe

Remove the barrel locating screw with a slotted screwdriver.

The barrel will now gently slide out of the block and the only task remaining before you can clean the barrel is to remove the silencer, which is simply achieved by loosening the holding screw on the base of the silencer and then sliding it off.

The barrel clamp screw.

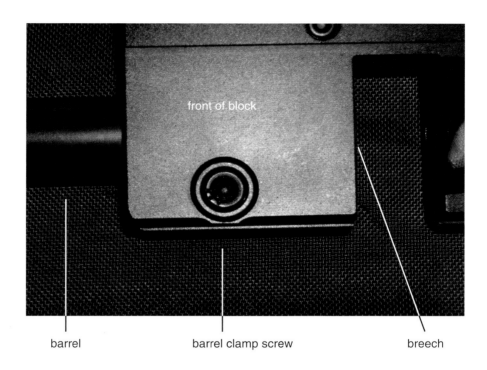

barrel   barrel clamp screw   breech

The barrel clamp screw.

Remove the barrel clamp screw and the barrel clamp

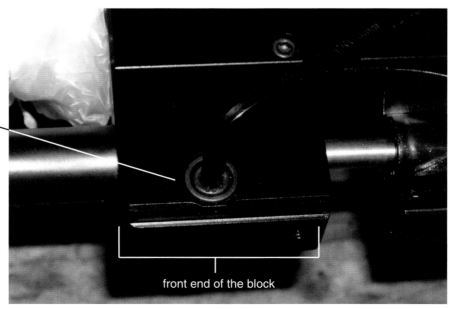

front end of the block

Remove the barrel clamp screw and the barrel clamp.

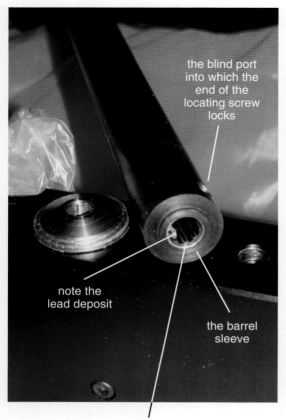

the blind port
into which the
end of the
locating screw
locks

note the
lead deposit

the barrel
sleeve

the barrel (note the lands and grooves)

The barrel removed.

The barrel can now be cleaned, and for this I recommend the Napier pull through, with Ultra Clean gun patches. The gun patches are a double-sided fabric on a 12m roll, the fabric is chemically inert so that it can be used with any cleaner or lubricant you like. On one side the Ultra Clean patches have a coarse finish, and when this side of the patch is drawn through the barrel it has a safe abrasive action that scrubs the bore clean; all the dirt and lead particles released by the coarse patch being trapped within the fibres, so that they are completely removed from the barrel. The other side of the Ultra Clean patches have a smooth finish and these are used in conjunction with the Napier gun lubricant, which is sprayed down the barrel, then the smooth side of the Ultra Clean patch is drawn down the barrel with the Napier pull through to spread the lubricant evenly and to remove any excess, giving the barrel its finishing touch.

Cleaning your rifle's barrel in this way will keep it clean but it will not strip all the lead from the barrel, so there is no need for

Removing the silencer.

The stock bolt.

underside of the stock

the stock bolt

trigger guard

re-leading. The Napier cleaning kit is the perfect choice for the serious airgun hunter who wants to ensure that the barrel does not lose accuracy through heavy fouling of the choke with lead or dirt. Unlike a rod, the pull through will not damage the choke because the patches, which the pull through drags down the barrel, are very flexible. When they reach the choke they simply become more compressed to pass through the choke, offering a high degree of cleaning but causing no damage. You have now successfully cleaned the barrel of your rifle and can refit it to the block by reversing the process that you have just gone through to remove it.

Let us now turn our attention to lubricating the trigger. To get at the trigger, first remove the stock, which is achieved by removing the single stock bolt located on the underside of the stock, just forward of the trigger.

This bolt should be kept lightly greased, using a white grease to keep it free moving, as you will find yourself removing the stock several times every month. Most rifles have a number of screws holding the stock to the action; some of the screws are small and difficult to get at, making the removal of the stock a fiddly job. The sensible approach taken by Theoben means that stock and action can be liberated from one another in seconds, making life a lot easier and gun maintenance a lot quicker.

When you reunite the stock and the action the stock bolt will have to be tightened to a specific torque, as too much or too little tightening of this bolt can have a detrimental effect on the rifle's accuracy. This is something that a lot of shooters would not think of, but it is attention to the minutiae that brings a weapon to the pinnacle of its potential as regards accuracy. As an exponent of long-range airgun hunting you will need to have an eye for such fine detail in order that you can fine-tune your weapon to its optimum potential.

The torque setting for the stock bolt is likely to vary from rifle to rifle, due to the individual nature of barrels, so try out a number of different torque settings on your rifle, testing the rifle on the range after each setting and see which torque setting produces the best grouping. From my experiments, and the experience of others, the rifle prefers to have the stock bolt on a light torque setting rather than being heavily tightened.

With the stock placed to one side you can now observe the underside of the block where the trigger is located and you will see that the trigger is held in place by two pins, a pin being a rod of metal.

Drive these pins out using a small punch of the correct diameter. The punch should be struck with an engineer's mallet using light blows, which are more than sufficient to drive out the pins. The action should be placed on a wooden block with a hole drilled into it, large enough to receive the pins when they are knocked out of the action. This ensures that you do not loose the pins and places the action, during the work process, on a surface that will not damage or mark metal. With the pins removed, you will find it easy to draw the trigger mechanism from the action, by pulling on the safety catch and gently working the trigger block back and forth in a rocking action to encourage it to slide away from its housing.

Inspect the trigger mechanism for dust and dirt, removing any that you find by blowing it out of the mechanism (with your own breath, not compressed air) or using a small modelling paintbrush to dislodge the offending particles. Once all the dirt is removed to

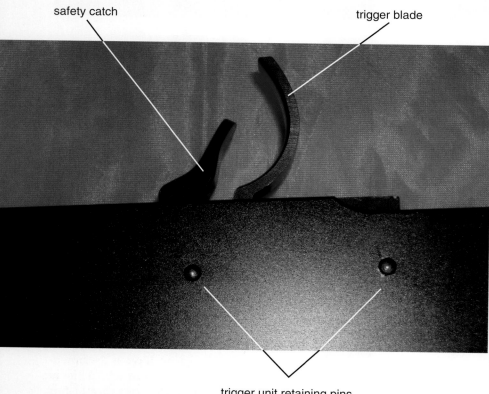

safety catch

trigger blade

trigger unit retaining pins

Trigger unit retaining pins.

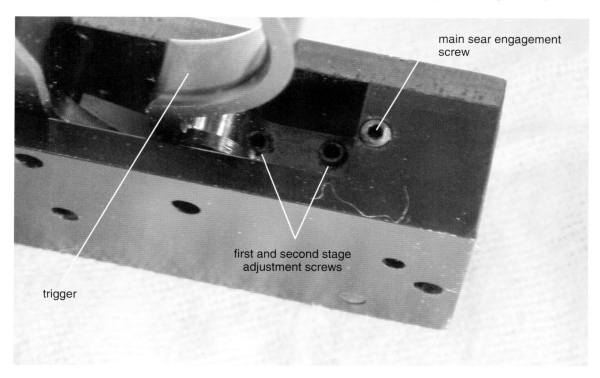

main sear engagement screw

first and second stage adjustment screws

trigger

The trigger mechanism.

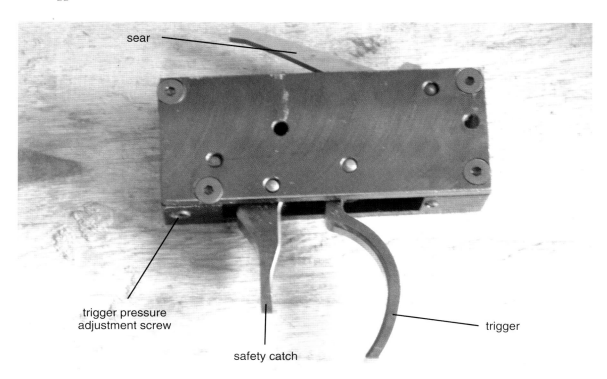

sear

trigger pressure adjustment screw

safety catch

trigger

A selection of trigger oils and silicone sprays.

your satisfaction, apply a few drops of good quality trigger oil, making sure that all the moving parts of the mechanism receive a light, even coating of oil. Abbey Lubricants, a specialist in the manufacture of gun lubricants, produce a good quality trigger oil or you can use three-in-one, which is a good quality, lightweight oil. Do not go mad with the oilcan, it is much better to lubricate little and often than to apply large amounts of lubricant rarely. Excessive amounts of lubricant, whether that is oil or grease, will attract contamination in the form of dust and dirt particles, which will turn the lubricant into an aggressive grinding paste that will rapidly wear down the surface of the metal.

When applying trigger oil, disengage the safety catch and depress the trigger half a dozen or so times to work the lubricant into all areas of the mechanism. And do not forget to re-engage the safety catch before returning the trigger block to the action.

The fact that trigger oil is produced by companies who specialize in the manufacture of gun lubricants, is evidence enough that the trigger of a weapon requires regular maintenance. Add to this the fact that professional gun users, such as snipers and police marksmen, regularly service the trigger of their weapon with oil, and you have proof that the neglect of the trigger's lubrication is detrimental to a weapon's performance. Neglect the trigger and it will dry out and become stiff and, slowly but surely, corrosion will creep into the mechanism and, what was once a great match grade trigger will become a poor excuse for a trigger that will cause the once tight groupings to open up.

I know that I am labouring the point a bit, but I am with the great soldier and military tactician, the Duke Of Wellington, who said to his troops regarding their muskets, do not spare the oilcan. Of course mineral-based oil on a PCP has to be kept confined to the correct areas of the weapon, as such oil in the regulator or air ports would, upon the release of a charge of air, cause an explosion. I am not sure if such an explosion would prove fatal to the shooter, but it would not be a pleasant experience and would ruin the rifle, so it is best avoided.

There is a general fear, for the reason mentioned above, of putting oil onto a PCP, but triggers need to be oiled and even the internal moving parts need to be lubricated. This is done when the weapon is serviced using specialist white grease, which is safe to use inside a compressed air system. Quite a few writers say that you do not need to lubricate your rifle, stating that it will work for many years without any attention whatsoever and maybe it will, but it will not work to its optimum potential. The argument that moving parts do not need lubricating is an argument against the laws of physics, which tell us about friction. Friction is the abrasive wearing down of two components that rub against one another in their cycle of movement, which is why lubricants were invented. Have a go at not putting lubricants into your car or lawn mower and see what happens: total and utter mechanical breakdown when the pistons seize up. And the same is true of a rifle; neglect its lubrication and you will face mechanical failure, which will be preceded by a steady and continuous decrease in performance. So oil and grease what needs to be oiled and greased on your rifle.

Some shooters have taken to applying molybdenum disulphide grease to the trigger action of their rifle but, to do this properly, you need to strip down the trigger unit and remove the old grease before applying the new coating. This is an awful lot of very fiddly work, just to lubricate a trigger, which can be lubricated just as well with a few drops of well-placed, well-chosen, oil.

Another problem with applying grease to the trigger unit is that if you over-apply the grease it will create drag, impeding the movement cycle of the trigger's moving parts, which is the very thing that you are trying to avoid by lubricating the trigger. Although a light grease will work on the trigger, I cannot see that it is a better choice than good quality oil.

Another part of a PCP that must be lubricated on a regular basis is the rubber O-rings placed around the neck of the buddy bottle. These O-rings create an airtight seal between the neck of the bottle and the rifle's regulator.

The rubber that these O-rings are made from is a natural substance and if not kept lubricated they dry out and crack. When this happens they are no longer able to create an airtight seal and your rifle will have a leak, which will result in air seeping from the barrel in varying degrees. This will affect both the power and accuracy of your weapon, making the rifle inconsistent – and all because a small rubber O-ring has perished.

Again you have to use the correct lubricant on the O-rings because they come into contact, although minimally, with compressed air and the wrong lubricant could cause an explosion. The correct lubricant for rubber O-rings is silicone grease which can be purchased in 600g tubs from Best Fittings, a company that specializes in the supply of spare parts and maintenance equipment for the servicing and repair of weapons-related air systems. A 600g pot of silicone grease will last a lifetime, as you apply silicone grease very sparingly to O-rings, as too much grease is as bad as no grease at all.

Silicone grease is made up of silicon and oxygen atoms, to which organic radicals are attached, producing grease that is not ignited when it comes into contact with compressed air. Some shooters think that silicone grease is a synthetic substance but silicon is, in fact, a natural, non-metallic element, found in its natural state as a brown or dark grey dust or as black crystals. Silicon is the second must abundant element

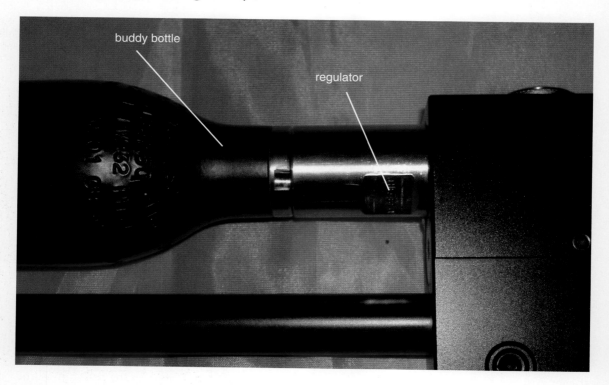

ABOVE: *The union between buddy bottle and rifle.* BELOW: *The O-ring on the neck of the buddy bottle.*

Parts of the bolt housing.

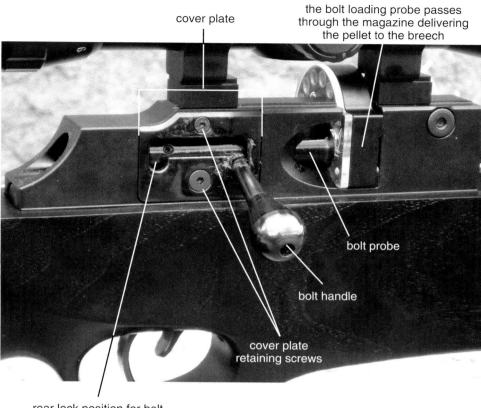

cover plate

the bolt loading probe passes
through the magazine delivering
the pellet to the breech

bolt probe

bolt handle

cover plate
retaining screws

rear lock position for bolt

in the earth's crust and has the scientific symbol Si.

The next part of the rifle that needs to be lubricated is the bolt. There are some rifles around with lever actions and I have owned some but never again; the lever is impossible to clean and nearly as impossible to lubricate. The one I had attracted dirt particles to the lever like a magnet attracts metal, so I shall never again own a weapon with a lever action. I consider the bolt action to be far superior, not just from a maintenance point of view, but also from the handling aspect, as levers are always small, fiddly, and hard to locate cocking devices. In comparison, the pear-shaped bolt handle fitted to the Theoben range of rifles is a chunky piece of metal that comes easily to hand for a quick and crisp movement of the bolt; even when wet and slippery this bolt handle is easily gripped.

A lot of airgun shooters simply slide the bolt back and lubricate the visible part of the bolt, considering this to be an adequate way to service the bolt with lubricant. However, in the world of firearms, the bolt is always completely removed from the action in order to clean and lubricate it. This was the way that I was taught to lubricate a bolt many years ago in the army cadets on a Lee Enfield 303, and it is the method that I still use, applying it now to air rifles. With the bolt removed, the bolt itself can be cleaned before lubrication, which is the correct way to apply fresh grease, while the chamber down which the bolt travels can be cleaned as well.

I have known some very expensive PCPs with bolt loading mechanisms, in which the bolt continually gave way to rust because the shooters were not lubricating the bolt

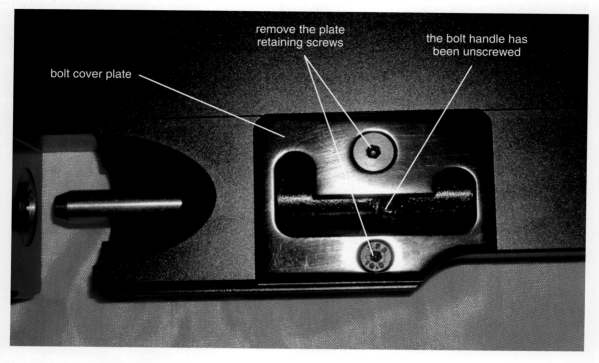

bolt cover plate

remove the plate
retaining screws

the bolt handle has
been unscrewed

Removing the bolt handle and cover plate.

correctly. Not all air rifles have the facility to remove the bolt from the action, but Theoben rifles do offer this facility using a design that is so simple it is pure genius. To extract the bolt, first remove the pear-shaped bolt handle, which is achieved simply by placing the correct-sized Allen key in the end of the bolt handle and turning it anti-clockwise, and the bolt handle will screw out.

You will now be looking at a cover plate held in place by two very small screws that, again, are rotated loose by means of an Allen key, allowing you to lift the plate.

With the plate removed you will now have a clear view of the bolt. Place an Allen key, or the end of a screwdriver, into the threaded hole into which the bolt handle screws; this will have the effect of rotating the bolt, bringing into view the lug which sets the hammer spring. This lug is secured to the bolt by a tiny little screw with a hex head. Loosen this screw with an Allen key and remove the lug, making sure that you do not lose the screw.

The bolt will now slide out in a rearwards direction.

Wipe all the old grease off the bolt using a clean, soft cloth, then wrap some cloth around a length of dowel of a suitable diameter and send it up and down the chamber in which the bolt travels, to clean away all the old grease and dirt. Re-lubricate the bolt with copper grease and reassemble, making sure that everything is securely fastened but not over-tightened. I can remove the bolt from my Theoben Tactical hunting rifle in less than thirty seconds, so it is easy to keep the bolt maintained in pristine condition. As this is such an easy operation, I remove the bolt after every hunting trip, then clean and re-lubricate it so that dirt and moisture do not have the slightest opportunity to build up around the bolt and establish a breeding ground for rust.

The last part of the rifle that needs to

Removing the lug.

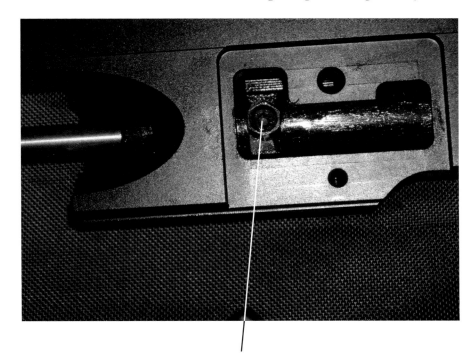

rotate the bolt to reveal the cocking lug which is removed by an Allen key

be lubricated is the outer metal surface of the block and barrel, simply as a means of preventing corrosion and to keep the metalwork clean and tidy. These days this is often done with a silicone impregnated cloth but, being old school, I see nothing wrong with a soft cloth that has been made nice and oily by applying generous amounts of three-in-one oil to it.

To oil the metalwork, remove the stock and run the cloth over the entire rifle, rubbing vigorously so as to drive the oil into the metal. There is no danger of this oil ending up where it should not if you place a completely empty magazine in the rifle and close the bolt, which will seal off the breech end of the barrel, ensuring that no mineral oil comes into contact with compressed air. One of the really annoying things about oiling the metalwork is that you just get it all nice and shiny, and then leave fingerprints all over the surface of the metal when you return the action to the stock. This can be avoided by wearing a cheap pair of cotton gloves, the kind that butlers wear to polish silverware.

Keeping the metalwork free from corrosion is not going to make the gun any more accurate, but it must be remembered that the outer surface of the gun, being the area most exposed to the elements, is going to be the first area to succumb to corrosion. Once corrosion has taken a hold it will spread like measles, getting into the internal parts of the gun, which will, in turn, affect accuracy and performance. If you have ever owned an old car that suddenly gives way to rust you will know what I mean; one minute there is a small speck of rust no bigger than a pin prick and then, before you know it, the red metal eater is breaking out all over the place. So, taking care of the outer surface of the gun is an essential maintenance procedure that will help to keep corrosion away from the weapon's vital internal components.

The Theoben rifles have an aluminium block and, although this is impervious to rust, it is not impervious to all forms of

with the lug removed the bolt will slide out

Removing the bolt.

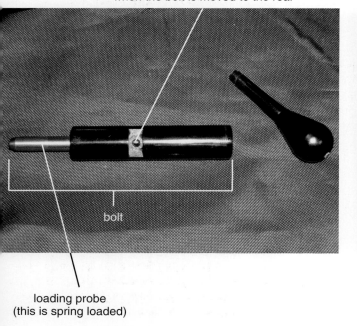

the thread for the cocking lug
which draws back the hammer
when the bolt is moved to the rear

bolt

loading probe
(this is spring loaded)

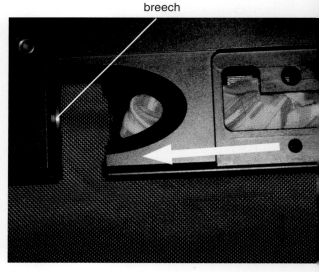

breech

push a clean piece of cloth down the
bolt chamber to remove old grease

corrosion. A lot of people think that because aluminium does not rust, it does not corrode but that is not the case at all. Aluminium can oxidize and, once that begins to happen it spreads very rapidly, pitting the surface. Although it does not eat through aluminium at anywhere near the rate that rust eats through steel, it does eventually undermine the aluminium, causing it to crack.

When an aluminium component oxidizes, a white fur-like substance appears on the surface; however, aluminium is very resistant to this corrosion as it has a naturally developed skin. This skin takes the form of an invisible oxide film that forms a barrier on the surface of the metal that corrosion cannot penetrate. This skin can be made even thicker by carrying out an electrolytic anodic oxidation treatment, known as anodizing, which is what Theoben do to the aluminium block on their rifles, making the block exceptionally resistant to corrosion. However, any deep scratches, even microscopic ones, can open up the protective skin, allowing the atmosphere to access the bare aluminium beneath. This is why even the block is oiled with an oil-soaked rag, so as to seal any scratches that have occurred, as is the barrel, as its protective coating can also be opened up by microscopic scratches.

The oil barrier is also necessary to provide a top layer or protection should blood or salt come into contact with the block, both of which are able to attack the protective coating. These contaminates have an even greater affect on the barrel protection, which is a film known as blueing, produced by a chemical reaction under the influence of heat.

Therefore, even though the block and the outer of the barrel on a Theoben precision hunting rifle are well protected, you cannot neglect them and so, each time that you return from a hunting trip, the oiled rag should be run over the metalwork. Treat a Theoben rifle with this kind of respect and it will literally last you a lifetime. Oiling the rifle in this way also means that you can carry out a visual inspection of the rifle after every outing, ensuring that any damage to the weapon is identified straight away.

Being an advanced airgun hunter is all about attention to fine detail and meticulous preparation, which means having your precision hunting rifle in perfect order at all times and fine-tuned to perfection to suit your specific needs. A dirty, poorly maintained rifle will never be up to the task of engaging live quarry at long range, no matter how well made the rifle. A precision, handmade hunting rifle is useless if not properly maintained, so do not harbour the idea that purchasing a top of the range gun is all that is required; intensive maintenance is essential. For the precision hunting rifle, deployed against long-range targets, maintenance and fine-tuning are its lifeblood.

As regards the oiling of any part of the rifle, it is worth mentioning that you should never apply oil to a rifle that is wet, even if you have dried it down with kitchen towel, as there will still be tiny drops of moisture lurking in fissures and hard to get at places; if you apply oil you will in fact seal in the damp making things worse, rather than better. The weapon needs to dry after it has got wet but do not place it next to a warm fire as, if you bring a metal object in from the cold and place it in a warm environment, you will cause it to sweat. By that I mean that condensation forms, heavily covering the entire rifle inside and out with a layer of moisture so, rather than drying it out, you actually soak it through more thoroughly than using it in the pouring rain. A wet gun should be removed from the stock, wiped down with an absorbent material like kitchen towel, then left in a safe place to dry that is not heated or damp, placing the rifle on blocks so that the air can circulate freely around it.

Forcing a rifle to dry rapidly by using heat can do more harm than good, just let it dry naturally at its own pace. If you have been meticulous with the oil cloth, then the outer surface of the rifle will be well sealed, with oil creating a water-repellent coating, just like wax on a car's bodywork, so there should be no threat of corrosion as long as the gun is properly dried out. If there is time to make a partial strip down of the weapon, then it will obviously dry more rapidly and parts of the gun that are inaccessible for drying will be revealed. By partial strip down I refer to the removal of the scope and mounts, the barrel and the silencer from the barrel; all of this dismantling, of course, following the removal of the action from the stock. A partial strip down of this nature can easily be achieved with the correct tools in five minutes, or less with practice.

In the military, recruits used to be taught how to strip and reassemble their personal weapon with a blindfold on. This is not a futile exercise as it is entirely possible that a soldier in action could find himself having to carry out a repair on his weapon in the dark, under fire, and so he must have total familiarity with it. The advanced airgun hunter should also have total familiarity with their weapon, so that they can maintain it to the standard required for long-range precision shooting.

Before moving on, let me just say a few words about stock maintenance. A quality walnut stock is just about one of the toughest pieces of wood you will come across. It will take a tremendous amount of abuse without failing; however, it will, due to the rugged nature of hunting in the countryside, get scratched and banged about quite badly over the years, damaging the protective coating, which is usually the application of a wood oil rather than the application of varnish. However, some of the Theoben guns, like the Tactical precision hunting rifle, have a stock with a paint finish.

Whatever the finish, once it has incurred scratching or grazing then the wood beneath is opened up to the elements and, whilst quality, well-seasoned walnut, such as that used by Theoben, will most likely last a lifetime, but where bare wood has been revealed it is important to keep a layer of protection over the top of it in order to guarantee its longevity. This is easily achieved by giving the stock a light coat of beeswax every few weeks. Beeswax will not only protect the stock but, where scratches have occurred, it will nourish the bare wood exposed by the scratch. I do not know why some gun manufacturers do not try applying a beeswax finish to their stocks, as it is a totally natural product that offers excellent protection, whilst feeding the wood and keeping it in prime condition.

When you have the stock removed from the action take a look at the inside of it and you will see that, even with a quality stock, the manufacturers do not give the inside surface the same protective layer that they apply to the outside. In fact some manufacturers leave the inner surface of the stock as bare wood, which is a bit naughty when you consider the price of quality rifles these days, so do not forget to give the inside surface of the stock a good coating with the beeswax.

Do not think that the inner surface of the stock, because it is hidden away from view, does not get exposed to moisture and dirt; in fact it is a magnet for both. For obvious reasons, the action is not sealed into the stock, so there is no watertight barrier to prevent rainwater running down the action and onto the inner surface of the stock where drainage is slow. This is why it is so important to remove the action from the stock after hunting in the rain, and why the inner surface of the stock should not be neglected. Some hunters say that they do not go out hunting in the rain which I find astonishing in the British Isles; if I were to take such a stance I would hardly ever get any hunting done up here on the north-east coast of Scotland.

You may think that I have over-laboured the subject of rifle cleaning, but I would disagree; there is a direct link between rifle maintenance and a weapon's accuracy. Only a well-maintained weapon will be able to operate as a precision hunter, so the advanced airgun hunter must have a thorough knowledge of the practical servicing procedures that need to be carried out on a regular basis.

BUILT-IN SUPPORT

As you will discover later on in this book, the long-range airgun hunter never takes a shot from an unsupported position; in other words, the shooter never simply uses the support of the human frame to steady the weapon, but seeks out ways to place the weapon into contact with a firm object, which will offer complete stability. That may mean placing the weapon in contact with the ground, or it may mean placing it in contact with some other object, such as the bonnet of a vehicle.

The problem is that where you need to take up your shooting position, there may not be a suitable object on which to rest the weapon, so it is very useful to have a built-in support system on the rifle, in the form of a bipod attached to the front of the weapon. A bipod, as the name suggests, is a two-legged, 'A'-shaped framework with telescopic legs that provides the rifle with a means of being placed in contact with the ground, at a level that aligns the gun with the shooter. Bipods come in two lengths; the prone bipod for use in the prone position, and the kneeling bipod for use in the kneeling and sitting positions.

My preference is for the prone position, which is the most stable platform the shooter can adopt. Generally speaking bipods are attached to a stud placed in the fore-end of the stock. The problem with this is that you tend to get a seesaw effect, where the bipod acts as a pivot about which the rifle can rock back and forth. Obviously this causes some degree of difficulty for the shooter trying to create a stable platform from which to discharge a shot.

If you take a look at the TPG 1, a tactical weapon for precision shooting at 1000yd which comes in 308 calibre, you will see that the fore-stock reaches just over one third of the way down the barrel, and the bipod is attached to the front of this far-reaching fore-stock. Now look at PCPs with a buddy bottle and you will see that the fore-stock on these guns generally ends marginally forward of the breech. The point is, the further down the weapon you are able to locate the bipod, the better platform it is able to provide in terms of stability.

At the Single Shot Black Powder Cartridge Rifle Club Of Great Britain, they use home-made wooden bipods in the shape of an x, which they position just a few inches back from the muzzle in the prone position, which offers a very stable support platform for these extremely powerful weapons. Again they are working on the principle of getting the support as far forward as possible. When using a rifle with a buddy bottle, which covers all the rifles in the Theoben range, then it is possible to place your bipod in a very effective forward position that eliminates the seesaw effect by using the buddy bottle itself as the location for the bipod; this is achieved by using a device simply called the buddy bottle bipod mount, manufactured by Best Fittings.

This mount is a metal collar that slides easily onto the buddy bottle and is then secured in place by turning the steel locking screw; do not go mad tightening this screw, all that is required is to create a firm closure of the clamp. Some shooters do not like the idea, fearing that they might over-tighten the mount and crush the buddy bottle. This is absurd, as, even if you could generate sufficient torque to accomplish this task, the head of the locking screw would shear off long before you began to crush the bottle.

The other argument against using a mounting system attached to the outer of the buddy bottle concerns the strain that is placed on the neck of the buddy bottle when the rifle is being carried over the shoulder on a sling, if the underside of the bipod is being used as the forward sling mount. I certainly hope that the neck of the buddy bottle on my gun is up to taking far more stress than could be induced by me walking the barrel of my gun into a tree branch whilst it is slung over my shoulder.

However, it is not really a concern for me as I do not use my bipod as the forward mount for my sling but have, in fact, adopted the military method of slinging my rifle, placing the studs in the side of the stock. The reason for this is that I often walk miles over rough terrain with the rifle slung over my shoulder. If the sling is secured to the underside of the stock you have the base of

The buddy bottle bipod mount from Best Fittings.

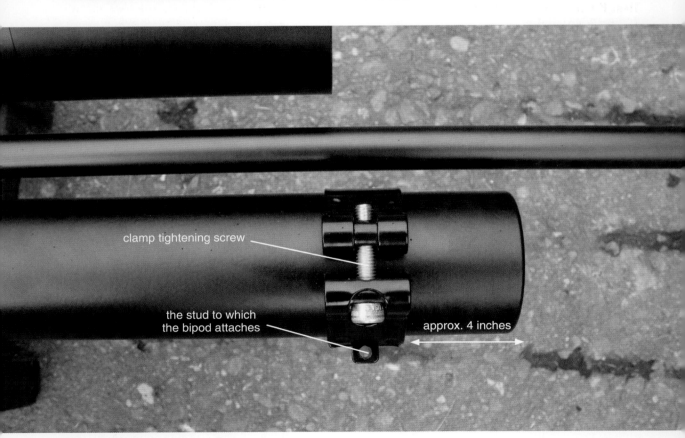

clamp tightening screw

the stud to which the bipod attaches

approx. 4 inches

Attach the mount roughly 4in back from the front of the bottle.

the pistol grip, which is very prominent on my Theoben Tactical, digging into the small of your back making it a very uncomfortable way to carry a rifle. Whereas when the studs are located in the side of the stock you have the flat surface of the side of the stock against your back and, whilst having the sling mounted on the side of the rifle may not look as pretty as having it mounted in the underside of the stock, my only concerns are my rifle's functionality and precision; mounting the sling on the side of the stock is the most functional set up that you can have, which is why it is the set-up used by the military.

Now that the bipod-mounting collar is attached securely to the buddy bottle it is time to attach a bipod. But which one of the many on the market makes the best buy for the long-range precision airgun hunter? Best Fittings now supply customized Debben tilting bipods. Why tilting? This is because the ground, which the legs of the bipod will be in contact with, is not usually level. This means that there will be a cant, which will cause the rifle to lean slightly to one side, making perfect eye alignment with the scope impossible. Cant will, as a result of poor eye alignment, cause the shot placement to be quite considerably off target. Cant can actually be seen as a dark shadow around the outer edge of the ocular lens.

The tilting bipod has a locking device which, when loosened, allows the rifle to tilt within a movable cradle on the top of the bipod so that, when the legs of the bipod are on uneven ground, the gun itself can move in order to gain a level position, allowing the eye to align perfectly with the scope. When making the adjustment to remove the cant, some shooters simply look down the scope and know when their rifle is level by the disappearance of the cant shadow. Other shooters actually have a spirit level attached to their rifle and know that the cant is removed when the bubble in the spirit level is reading level.

Once the cant has been removed, the locking device on the bipod is moved back to the locked position. The standard Deben bipod uses a very small knurled wheel as the means of operating the locking device, which is very fiddly, hard to find, and uncomfortable to operate: however this is the only design flaw in an otherwise excellent bipod. Best Fitting have customized the Deben bipod by removing that nasty little knurled wheel and replacing it with a large lever that is easy to find and operate, even in the dark, thus turning an excellent bipod into a perfect bipod and it is the one that I would recommend.

If you do not have a bipod then buy one direct from Best Fittings. If you already have a Deben bipod with the knurled wheel I mentioned, then contact Best Fittings and they will supply you with a replacement lever, which you can fit yourself. To attach the bipod to the stud on the base of the buddy bottle bipod mount, loosen the bipods locking screw, which allows the jaws of the stud clamp to open. It is then a matter of getting the lugs at the top of the clamp's jaws to go through the hole in the stud. When this happens, tighten the bipod's locking screw, making sure that the bipod is level. You will not be able to fully tighten the locking screw by hand, so give it a few turns with a Phillips screwdriver to achieve the required level of torque to ensure that it is secure.

The instructions for fitting a bipod tell you to hold the bipod straight but, as you will discover when you fit your bipod, they have a mind of their own and will always favour tightening to one side, despite your most valiant efforts to keep them straight, which is another reason why you need a tilting bipod as opposed to a fixed one. With a fixed bipod there is nothing you can do to compensate for the fact that the bipod has tightened off to one side, rendering it incapable of offering a level platform from which to fire. Out to about 30yd you may well get away with this if you are only looking for a 1in grouping, but at 40yd wishing to achieve a 12mm grouping, a bipod that is not level is going to give you some trouble.

With a tilting bipod, the fact that it is has tightened off to one side making the rifle lean ever so slightly, can be compensated for

The effect of cant.

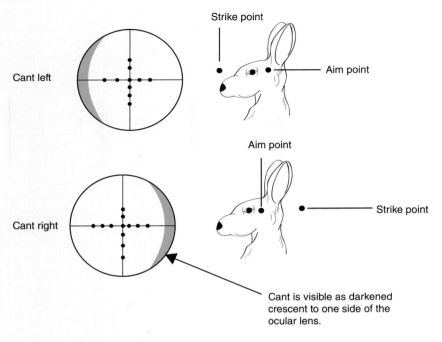

Cant = An inclination from the level

Strike point

Aim point

Cant left

Aim point

Cant right

Strike point

Cant is visible as darkened crescent to one side of the ocular lens.

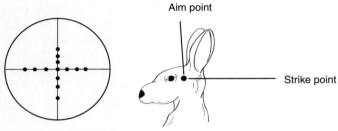

Aim point

Strike point

Slight almost imperceptible cant will result in non-fatal wounding.

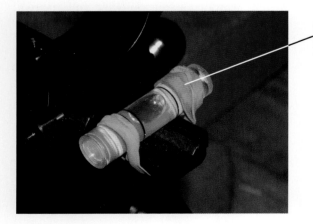

the level is simply held on with a rubber band

Spirit level mounted to the Weaver rail used to remove cant.

*The Best Fittings
lever refit.*

the Best Fittings bipod lever

by loosening the locking device and levelling the rifle using a rifle-mounted spirit level which we shall look at in the chapter on the scope. If you have studied this chapter carefully and studied your rifle equally carefully, you should now have the knowledge to set up your rifle to perfection for long-range shooting.

You may think that this chapter is a bit long and detailed, but the fact of the matter is that the rifle properly set equals at least forty per cent of the equation for achieving a long-range shot; setting up the scope

correctly will account for about twenty per cent and the shooter's technique the remaining forty per cent.

If you cannot get the rifle set up right then you will be missing nearly half the equation and success will be impossible, so study this chapter thoroughly until you understand your rifle and what needs to be done to it to make it work in harmony with your body and your abilities. When shooting, you and your gun should melt together into a seamless union that produces deadly accurate and consistent shooting.

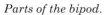

Parts of the bipod.

tension screw

this opening for a
sling swivel

release lever that
allows the cradle to
tilt on the horizontal
plane

legs fold
forward

spring loaded
adjustable legs

The correctly fitted adjustable bipod.

Chapter 2
The Scope For Precision Long-Range Airgun Hunting

CHAPTER OBJECTIVES

Knowledge:

With this chapter you will gain knowledge regarding the alignment of the scope with the bore of the rifle and the eye of the shooter: the key components to the successful use of a scope as a precision aiming device. The chapter will also show how to use the ½ mil dot reticle as a precise range-finding tool.

Practical Ability:

This chapter will acquaint you with the skills required to fix scope mounts to a rifle, and the scope into the mounts so that the cross hairs are lined up accurately with the bore.

Time period required to develop the practical skills:

Ten to fifteen hours.

THE EXIT PUPIL

In the last chapter we looked at the Theoben precision hunting rifle in great detail in order to understand how to set the rifle up for long-range shooting. The same principle holds true for the scope, as only the hunter with a deep knowledge of these very sophisticated sighting devices will be able to use them to optimum effect.

The exit pupil is the source of the image we see when we look into the ocular end of a rifle scope. It is the light travelling through the centre of the lenses within the scope,

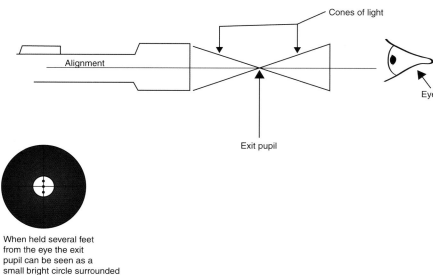

The exit pupil.

When held several feet from the eye the exit pupil can be seen as a small bright circle surrounded by darkness

first the objective lens, then the lenses in the erector tube, and finely the ocular lens and then onto our eye, positioned behind the scope. If you hold a scope at arm's length and then look into the ocular lens you will see, in the very centre of the lens, a circle surrounded by darkness; that small circle is the exit pupil.

In order to achieve consistent shot placement, the pupil of your eye must be placed in precise alignment with the exit pupil, in exactly the same location behind the scope, shot after shot. This means the same distance from the rear of the scope, known as eye relief (and which we shall consider shortly), and the exact same placement of the cheek on the stock every single time you take a shot.

This point cannot be stressed strongly enough; move the eye fractionally backwards or forwards, up or down, and you will have a different alignment with the exit pupil, resulting in a different strike point on the target. If you do not believe me then try it for yourself on a paper target, varying the position of your eye in relation to the exit pupil; the result will be the movement of the strike point.

You may think that the eye should be aligned with the centre of the cross hairs, and so it should, but if the scope has been properly set up the cross hairs will be in the centre zone of the exit pupil. In Chapter One we looked at variance; the rifle's ability to be consistent and to do the same thing over and over again to exactly the same measure. For precision shooting to become a reality you, the shooter, must also have the ability to do exactly the same thing over and over again, to the same measure, and with particular emphasis on the consistent placement of the eye in alignment with the exit pupil of the scope.

It does not matter how big and expensive the scope is, if you fail to master this basic action. Placing your eye in the same place every time involves having a consistent stock weld, which is the point at which the cheek meets the stock. If you have trouble placing your eye in the correct position every time then you could try placing a length of tactile tape on the stock, at the point where the cheek should be: the leather tape that they use on bicycle handlebars would work well. You may well need the help of an assistant to place the tape in the correct location as it will involve having the stock in the shoulder, with correct stock weld and eye alignment before the tape can be lined up. When placed on the stock the tape will act as a marker that you can feel with your cheek.

With the tape on the stock, spend hours on the range bringing the stock into the shoulder, each time feeling the tape against the cheek to see if the alignment is correct. Eventually, after sufficient practice, your muscles will become programmed and the eye and the cheek will go into the same place every time instinctively. It may, however, take tens of hours of practice to achieve the kind of consistency required for long-range shooting which requires, above all, total dedication. One of the other fundamental requirements for those wishing to become advanced airgun hunters is the dedication to spend hour upon hour on the range, honing the basics like eye alignment to perfection. Until you can master that, long-range shots will always be beyond your ability.

Another reason why the eye needs to be aligned with the exit pupil is because the exit pupil is the source of the scope's brightness. The clearest image is therefore to be viewed in the centre of the objective lens, so the eye must be lined up with the centre of the lens. If your eye is off to one side of the exit pupil the image you receive will be duller and thus clarity will be impaired. Brightness is much more important than magnification: if the image that you see lacks clarity it does not matter how large it is. The clear identification of the quarry's anatomical features to confirm the aim point is vital to a successful kill, especially in areas of low light. Therefore alignment of the eye with the exit pupil of the scope is imperative to achieve, not only the same aim point, but also a clear crisp image of the quarry.

The size of the exit pupil varies from

scope to scope, and can be calculated by dividing the diameter of the objective lens by the magnification of the scope. For example, a scope with a 42mm objective lens set on 6× magnification will have an exit pupil of 7mm. In dim light conditions, the pupil of a young adult will open to 7mm and, as a person gets older, the pupil's ability to open diminishes down to about 4mm or less. There is no point in having a scope with a bigger exit pupil than the opening capacity of the eye because the eye cannot draw in and hold more light than its capacity and therefore any excess light simply goes to waste.

When selecting a scope bear in mind that the bigger the exit pupil, up to the cut-off point of your eye's capacity, the brighter the image that you will see in the ocular lens. This is an important consideration because much of the hunter's quarry is taken in low light conditions when animals such as rabbits are most active: in early morning, at sundown, or actually in the dark with the aid of a light. The clarity of a small target like a rabbit at a distance of 40yd is very important; you simply cannot place the shot if you cannot clearly see the target, so the bigger the exit pupil the better.

Many hunters make the mistake of believing that the biggest magnification will give them the clearest image of the target quarry. However, as the magnification increases, the exit pupil decreases and so a scope with a 42mm objective, set at 6× magnification to create a 7mm exit pupil, if it were taken up to 20× magnification the exit pupil would actually go down to 2.1mm – a dramatic shrinkage that will significantly diminish the amount of brightness present at the ocular lens, thus compromising clarity. So bigger magnification does not mean a clearer image – it just means a bigger image and even if you had a huge scope with a 56mm objective lens, set at 20× magnification, you would still only have an exit pupil of 2.8mm.

The brightest and clearest images are to be had at the lower end of the magnification scale, so do not become obsessed with large magnification. In America some hunters

shoot Prairie Dogs from a considerable distance because the animals are so alert in an environment with no cover for the hunter. They therefore shoot from a distance of 1000yd, which is far in excess of anything an airgun hunter will ever do; for this extremely long-range shooting they use a scope with 10× or 14× magnification.

Hunters who turn their scopes up to 18× or 24× magnification are going over the top as, when the magnification is taken too high, clarity suffers. For long-range airgun hunting out to ranges of 40yd, a magnification of 9× to 12× is the optimum choice to bring the image up to sufficient size to see what you are aiming at, whilst still maintaining the exit pupil at a size that is able to bring about an acceptable level of brightness and clarity.

Whilst on the subject of brightness, it is worth mentioning that if you are carrying out night shooting operations using a light to target your quarry, the smaller the magnification you opt for, the brighter the image will be in the ocular lens. A setting of 6× magnification on a scope with an objective lens of 42mm will give an exit pupil of 7mm, but when that magnification is taken up to 12× magnification that figure drops to 3.5mm, halving the level of brightness.

If you want to hunt at night with a high level of magnification then you need to have the biggest objective lens you can get, which means a 56mm objective. With such a lens you could set the magnification at 12× and have an exit pupil of 4.6mm; this does provide an acceptably bright image but not as bright as that being produced by the 42mm scope set at 6× magnification. You could produce a much brighter image by turning the 56mm scope down to 6× magnification, but this would result in an exit pupil of 9.3mm that is producing far more light than the human eye can handle. The 42mm scope at 6× magnification offers the maximum light transmission that the human eye can handle. You therefore have to wonder if it is actually worth having a scope with a huge objective lens for night hunting; personally I believe that the variable scope with a 42mm objective lens is

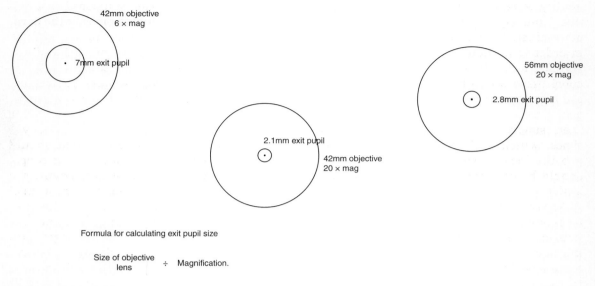

Formula for calculating exit pupil size

Size of objective lens ÷ Magnification.

The size of the exit pupil.

the best all round choice for the long-range airgun hunter.

CLEAN LENSES FOR CLARITY

Cleaning the scope's lenses is vital, as the thinnest film of dust covering the objective lens will compromise the brightness of the image considerably, and yet it is something that a lot of hunters never think about. There is no maintenance to speak of when it comes to scopes, you certainly do not apply oil to the turrets in the belief that it will keep them turning as quite the opposite is in fact true; scopes do not need lubrication, but they do need to have their lenses cleaned after every single hunting trip to keep them crystal clear.

The cleaning of the objective and ocular lenses is not a complex job, but it must be done properly or the lenses will be damaged. When I first started shooting I was guilty of using an old rag I carried around in my jacket pocket to wipe the lenses whenever they became covered in dust, or when spots of rain made viewing impossible. However

old rags are themselves contaminated with microscopic particles of dirt and will actually damage the lenses. You need special cloths for lens cleaning that have been manufactured for the purpose, and they need to be kept free from contamination by being stored in a sealed plastic bag.

However, you should not use the lens cloth before applying pressurized air to the lenses to blow away the dust and tiny particles of grit that will be present on the surfaces. If you did not blow away the grit first, when you use the lens cloth you will actually be rubbing the grit across the lens, which has much the same effect as using a mild abrasive; you will scratch the anti-reflection coating applied to the lenses and, although you will not be able to see the scratches, they will most certainly be there, and where these tiny little microscopic scratches occur, the light that is supposed to go through the scope will be reflected back, diminishing the clarity of the image.

When taking your sport to the next level, by extending the range at which you are going to engage quarry, you need to have equipment that is of the highest quality working at the peak of its capabilities. Your equipment therefore needs to be maintained to the very highest level and, in order to do that, you have to know what you are doing. If you do not have access to compressed air to blow away the dirt from the lenses, (and you will obviously not have access to it in the field whilst out hunting), then simply blow on the lenses several times, which will displace the dust, then rub the lenses over with a lens cloth you should be carrying about your person in a sealed plastic bag.

Alternatively, you could use a lens brush to remove the dust and then rub with a lens cloth. Never apply any window cleaning agents to the lenses as they are likely to damage the lens coating; if you do wish to clean your lenses with a fluid there are special lens cleaning fluids available for the purpose. It is amazing how many experienced hunters fail to keep the lenses of their rifle scope clean and, consequently, the scope is considerably less bright and clear than it is capable of being. So, pay very close attention to your lenses, as serious precision shooting requires a crystal clear image of the target.

EYE RELIEF

Eye relief is the distance that has to exist between the back of the scope and your eye in order for the full field of view to be visible. What the shooter needs to understand is that attaining the correct eye relief is critical; get it wrong and you will diminish the quality of the image that you have available through the ocular lens because the eye will be in the incorrect place in relation to the exit pupil.

The distance that the eye should be from the eye bell will appear in the literature that comes with a scope; if you wish to check that the stated eye relief is correct you can measure it using a strip of card and a small torch. Fold the end of the card up and then place the piece of card behind the scope. Next, shine the torch through the objective lens and then move the piece of card back

and forth until the beam is focused as a pinprick of light on the folded piece of the card. Measure the distance from the rear of the eye bell to the folded piece of card and you have the eye relief for that scope.

One of the top scope writers in America carries out this test with all his scopes and finds that some manufacturers give a false figure for eye relief; however, if you buy a good scope, such as a Hawke, that should not be the case. When mounting a scope, eye relief is generally set by eye, moving the scope back and forth along the rings until the full field of view is observed. However there is no harm in measuring from the rear of the eye bell to the eye to see if you are actually at the specified distance for eye relief. This is not to difficult to do if the rifle is completely supported in some way, as it needs to be to set the scope up for precision long-range shooting.

Eye relief, just like the exit pupil, changes with the level of magnification applied: the higher the magnification the shorter the eye relief, which means that if you set up your scope at 6× magnification and the eye relief is 3½in, when you turn up the magnification to 10× the eye relief will shrink to 3in, which means that when you turn up the magnification you need to place the eye closer to the ocular lens in order to receive the clearest image possible.

This feature has quite a useful side effect in that a scope has to be set up for one particular shooting position, when setting up a scope for precision shooting, which usually occurs with the shooter seated at a bench with the rifle supported on shooting bags. However, when the shooter adopts a prone position, the head is naturally moved forward, placing the eye too close to the scope for the eye relief that was set up in the sitting position. However, by increasing the magnification it is possible to shorten the eye relief, thus establishing the correct eye relief for the prone position. If the standing position is adopted, then the head moves away from the rear of the scope and this can be compensated for by reducing the level of magnification. If a rifle is set up on a bench

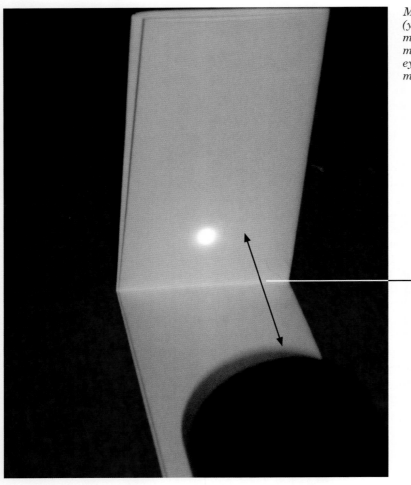

Measuring a scope's eye relief (you can carry out this form of measuring on different levels of magnification to find out what eye relief is necessary for specific magnification settings).

slide the piece of paper back and forth till the beam of light is perfectly focused

Measuring eye relief

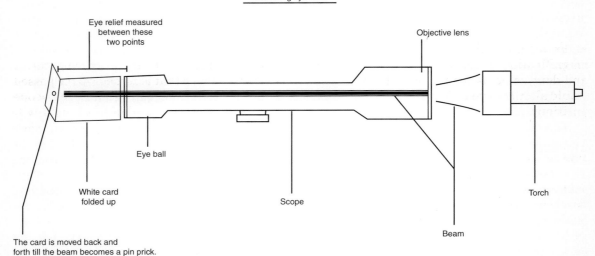

Eye relief measured between these two points

Objective lens

Eye ball

White card folded up

Scope

Torch

Beam

The card is moved back and forth till the beam becomes a pin prick.

The effect of magnification on eye relief.

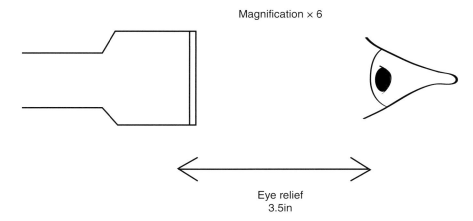

Magnification × 6

Eye relief
3.5in

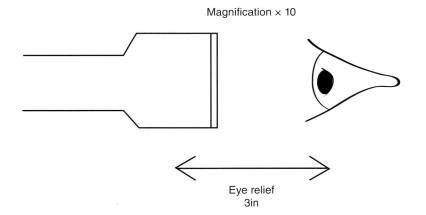

Magnification × 10

Eye relief
3in

(This is an example. Different scopes will exhibit different degrees of adjustment)

at 9× magnification, then increasing that magnification to 12× for the prone position and decreasing 6× for the standing position would alter the eye relief to suit the different positions.

FOCUSING THE SCOPE

Just a quick word about focusing the scope: it is surprising how many hunters forget to do this most basic of tasks. Scopes are zeroed to the rifle, that is to say that the cross hairs are aligned with the ballistic flight path created by the rifle's bore, but they are focused to the eye of the shooter. A rifle with a scope that is zeroed can be passed from one shooter to another and the scope will be zeroed for both shooters, but it will not be focused for both shooters unless they have very similar vision. Plenty of shooters set up their scope with the correct distance of eye relief, but they still do not get a clear image via the ocular lens and they wonder what they have done wrong. Many even go out hunting like this thinking that the image they are receiving is the best available and all they have failed to do is turn the ring

The focus ring.

focus ring

MOUNTING THE SCOPE FOR PRECISION SHOOTING

The Weaver System

In this book I shall only be looking at the use of Weaver mounts as I consider this particular system of mounting a scope to be the most superior available to the airgun hunter. I am astonished that so few airgun hunters make use of the Weaver system, as it is the most versatile system that you can have on your rifle. The Weaver system consists of a rail with channels machined into it at regular intervals along its length, and these channels engage with a bar located in the base of the scope mounts.

The purpose behind the design is to resist the movement created by the serious recoil offered by firearms, but as we are using a PCP with no perceptible level of recoil, this particular feature is an irrelevance. I think this is why so many airgun hunters overlook the Weaver system, as they see its only virtue being its ability to resist recoil, but there is so much more to the system than that. The entire range of Theoben PCPs can be fitted with a Weaver rail and, as you can see from the following photo, the mount extends several inches to the rear of the block and it covers the area above the magazine, meaning that it offers more surface area on which to mount the scope, then dovetails, giving greater latitude of adjustment.

How often have you set up a scope on a rifle and found that there is insufficient movement of the scope to get the eye relief spot on, with the front mount positioned right at the back of the forward section of the block, just barely hanging on and with the scope turrets right up against the rear mount, allowing not another fraction of a millimetre in adjustment. This is the frustrating reality with all the rifles that I have ever used, but when you fix a Weaver rail to your

at the rear of the eye bell, aptly named the focus ring. So do not forget to move the focus ring in and out to find the clearest possible view that you can achieve, or you will be operating with a scope that is out of focus with your eye making precision shooting impossible.

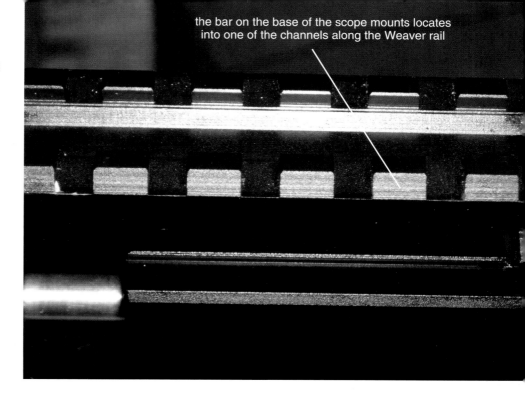

the bar on the base of the scope mounts locates into one of the channels along the Weaver rail

The Weaver rail and mounts.

rifle the problem disappears and you can set up the scope much more precisely, getting a better eye relief than can be achieved with standard mounts on a Dovetail.

Any rifle can be fitted with a Weaver rail using an adaptor kit that fits to the Dovetail. These are available from Deben but the Theoben rifles are designed to take a Weaver rail that is actually screwed to the block, which is the preferable option. A single screw through the front and rear of the rail attaches it to the block and under the rail you can place raisers of different depths to allow for scopes with huge objective lenses, but do not forget that the closer the scope is to the rifle the easier it is to zero in the cross hairs.

The other great benefit with the Weaver system is that you can remove the scope with the greatest of ease and then reattach it in exactly the same place that it came from, meaning that the scope retains its zero, unlike the Dovetail system; once a scope is

Note the bar in the base of the mount which locks into the channels on the rail.

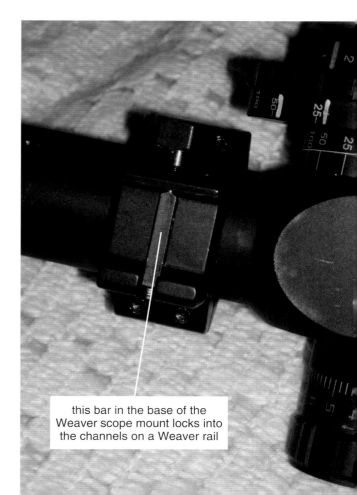

this bar in the base of the Weaver scope mount locks into the channels on a Weaver rail

removed from that, unless you have marked up the block, you will not be able to place it back precisely on the zero point.

Sniper rifles and the rifles of police marksmen are set up with a Weaver system and, when the weapon is not in use, the scope is removed with the mounts still attached and stored in a suitable case where it is protected from damage and the environment. When the rifle is required the scope is simply remounted back onto the same spot it came from, retaining zero, although a practice shot or collimator will be used to ensure that this is the case.

The Weaver system is therefore my preferred option for advanced airgun hunting. The scope has to be removed after every hunting trip in order to carry out basic rifle maintenance and, like the military and the police, I like to store my scope away when not in use. It is a precision instrument and needs to be well looked after to maintain its high level of precision. Hawke optics provide their top of the range scopes with a briefcase-type box with metal edging and a foam lining; this is where your scope should be kept when not in use and not on top of your rifle.

Fixing The Base Of The Scope Mounts To The Rail

In order to mount a scope for precision long-range shooting, you need to place the rifle on a table. Then, using shooting bags, support the rifle in such a way that it is perfectly level; place a small spirit level on the block checking both the horizontal and the parallel. If the rifle is not straight from the outset, then no matter how much care you take mounting the scope you will never achieve the required level of precision; having the rifle completely level is the foundation on which everything else is built. For normal airgun hunting such precision is not essential, but when you want to push the sport to its absolute boundaries everything must be perfect.

If you have the available funds you can get yourself a state-of-the-art shooting bench which will enable you to mount and zero the scope with more precision then you have ever managed to achieve before, simply because the bench provides the rifle with a stable platform on which to sit whilst you carry out the necessary work. A small adjustable seat attached to the bench allows you to sit behind the rifle and, with it supported by shooting bags, you can look down the scope without any body contact occurring which would, no matter how steady the contact, cause the rifle to be slightly off the level. Having the rifle held in this way allows you to bore sight the scope and ensures that there is not the slightest amount of cant.

A shooting bench is such a splendid piece of kit that, if you do not have one, you should add it to your wish list of shooting accessories. Shooting benches, however, are not cheap and if you would rather spend the £150 or more that such a bench would cost on your rifle and scope combination, then that is quite understandable. If you do not have a shooting bench then set up your mounts and scope with the rifle held perfectly still and level in a vice of some type, making sure that you cover the jaws of the vice with leather, rubber or some other kind of material that will prevent the jaws biting into the rifle. If you have no shooting bench then you can carry out the zeroing process in the prone position if you have fitted an adjustable bipod. This will enable you to use the bipod to support the front of the rifle and a homemade shooting bag to support the stock, adjusting both bipod and shooting bag until the rifle is perfectly level.

A homemade shooting bag is simply a plastic bag filled with the required amount of sand that is then double wrapped and taped to prevent the sand escaping. If you do most of your long-range shooting from the prone position then there is an obvious advantage in zeroing the rifle in that position as the rifle is then calibrated specifically to ensure precision in that shooting position.

With your rifle well supported and completely level on a shooting bench, or in a vice, it is time to attach the Weaver base rail. The Weaver rail screws directly to the

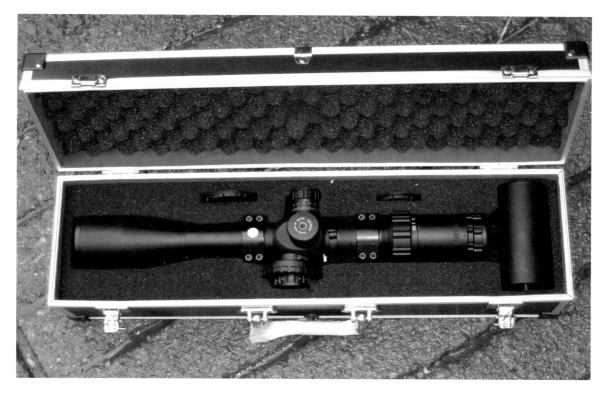

The protective case provided with top of the range Hawke scopes.

top of the block on a Theoben hunting rifle so nothing could be more simple, but do not over-tighten the screws and, once the rail is secured in place, use a spirit level to see that it is exactly level. If it is slightly off level then try adjusting the screws to see if you can get it level, simply because if one screw is tighter than the other it could very slightly cant the rail. If the level shows that the rail is seriously off the level then you have some kind of structural problem with your rifle and should get a gunsmith to take a look. To attach the bottom rings of the scope mount to the rail first, take your scope and hold it alongside the rail to give you an idea of where you need to place the bottom rings on the rail.

Place the bottom rings on the rail, engaging the bar in the bottom rings with the desired channel in the rail, then before tightening the rings in place, lay the scope across them and sit down behind the rifle, with your shoulder just touching the stock, and move the scope back and forth until you achieve the correct level of eye relief. If you cannot get the correct level of eye relief then move the bottom rings to another position and repeat this step. Once you are sure the bottom rings are in the right place for the correct eye relief to be achieved, place the scope safely to one side and tighten up the bottom rings. Again do not over-tighten; in fact with a PCP there is no need to go beyond hand tightening the base of the scope mounts, which makes it very easy to affix and remove the mounts and consequently the scope.

Now place your spirit level across the top of the rings to make sure there is not the slightest cant. If the level shows the existence of cant then make adjustments to the screw holding the ring in place, which should bring about a levelling of the ring. You might not think that tiny adjustments to the amount of tightening applied to the base of the scope mounts will have any impact at all on the level; however, even the slightest over-tightening can cause a cant of a fraction of a degree. In most branches of engineering, every fixing that needs to be on the level has a specified torque setting to ensure that over tightening does not bring about a cant; it is therefore important that you get away from the general trend to tighten fixings with the greatest amount of force that can be exerted. Once both bases have been secured to the rail and are level, place the scope into them and place a level on the flat part of the scope located on the top of the elevation turret (with the cap removed on models fitted with a cap).

Although you have ensured both base mounts are level there could be a slight imperfection in the ring part of the base where the scope sits; this area has to be completely smooth and both mounts have to match one another identically or the scope will be minutely off the level. The best way to avoid imperfections, which are the result of inaccurate machining, is to buy the very best mounts on the market. In the case of air rifle shooting this means mounts from Sports Match UK who manufacture mounts to a phenomenally high level of tolerance; the mounts are identical and therefore offer a perfectly level cradle in which the scope can sit.

If you decide to opt for cheap mounts, the only way to take out imperfections if they do not match up exactly is to file them down using a device called a lapping tool, which will cost you more than buying top-quality mounts. We are now at the stage where the bases are affixed and level and so we can now proceed to clamp the scope into the mounts; however, before we do this, the scope should be centred. Centring means placing the cross hairs in the centre of the exit pupil, which is a simple process that surprisingly few shooters carry out when mounting a scope and so the bore and cross hairs are poorly aligned, making the zeroing process a drawn out, frustrating affair.

To centre the cross hairs turn each turret, it does not matter in which direction, until it stops turning. When you come to the end of its cycle do not force it or you could damage the springs that move the cross hairs. Now turn the turret in the other direction, counting the number of clicks it makes until it will turn no further. Divide the number of clicks by two, then turn the turret that number of clicks, which will place the cross hairs dead centre. This process must obviously be performed with both the elevation and windage turrets.

Now place the scope in the base of the scope mounts; sit behind the rifle with your shoulder just touching the stock and move the scope back and forth until the correct level of eye relief is achieved. You will know when the correct eye relief is achieved because you will be able to see the full field of view in the ocular lens, and the entire lens will present a clear image with no dark shading around the outside. If you are not sure that the eye relief is correct, measure the distance from the ocular lens to your eye and see if the reading is the same as the eye relief which will be specified somewhere in the scope owner's manual. Once the eye relief has been set, place the scope mount's top rings over the scope and tighten them down until there is just enough tension to hold the scope in place, but not so tight that the scope cannot be moved slightly. The tightening sequence for the ring screws is left hand rear, right hand front, right hand rear, and left hand front: carrying out the same sequence for both rings. With this done check that the eye relief is still perfect.

Now we move to a process called bore sighting, which is an examination to see if the centre of the bore and the vertical cross hair are lined up. This check can only be carried out on a rifle where the bolt can be easily removed, which precludes most air rifles, but not the Theoben range which have a rapid bolt removal facility. For bore sighting remove the bolt from the Theoben, as explained in Chapter One, (this is best done before you start to mount the scope, so that you do not disturb the scope whilst the final adjustments are being made). Sit down behind the rifle held in a vice with the

The rifle held perfectly still in a vice.

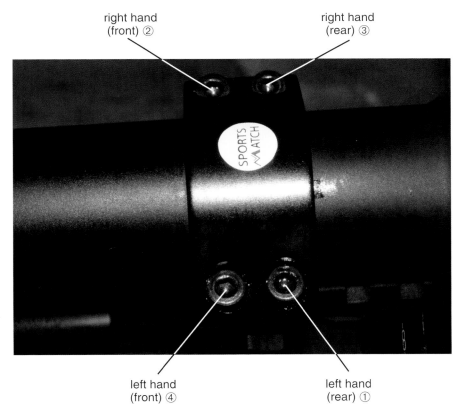

The tightening sequence.

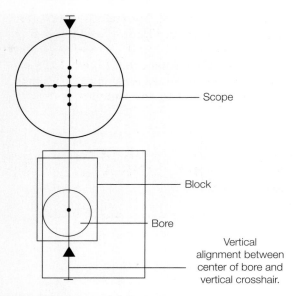

Scope

Block

Bore

Vertical
alignment between
center of bore and
vertical crosshair.

Bore alignment of the scope.

stock removed and you will be able to look through the back of the block and down the bore and through the ocular lens of the scope at the same time. If you draw an imaginary line vertically up the centre of the bore, this should line up with the vertical cross hair, meaning that they are aligned; if this is not the case then move the vertical cross hair to the left or right using the windage turret to align it with the centre of the bore.

Do not replace the bolt until you have finished securing the scope in place; there is then one last check to ensure that the cross hairs are perfectly straight. Even the slightest cant, imperceptible to the human eye, is sufficient to make precision alignment impossible, the pellet therefore being delivered to the side of the desired aim point. No amount of fiddling with the turrets will correct the fault, the cross hairs have to be as straight as a die or they do not provide an accurate aiming grid.

To test the cross hairs for straightness you only need to test one of them; if one is straight then the other, by virtue of their relationship, also has to be. The easiest of the cross hairs to test is the vertical one and the test can be carried out by making

a tripod out of three bamboo canes, held together at the top by a piece of string, and placed directly in front of the rifle at a distance of 10 to 15yd. Have the scope's parallax set at 10 or 15yd and bring its magnification down to 6×. From the tripod suspend a plumb line, which will hang true. Now sit behind your rifle and look through the scope and align the vertical cross hair with the plumb line by rotating the tube as required.

There is another method that can be used which bore sights the scope and also checks that the cross hairs are completely straight, using a device that fits into the end of the barrel called a collimator. This is a calibration tool and, whilst these devices are quick and easy to use, they generally cost £50 or more but I have not yet seen one that does .25 and .20 calibre.

The scope is now perfectly level with straight cross hairs that are aligned to the bore, so you can tighten the top rings down using the tightening sequence mentioned above. It is imperative that you use the tightening sequence to apply evenly distributed torque as an uneven distribution of torque will result in a canting of the scope, ruining all the precision mounting work that you have done up to this point. The importance of having the scope correctly mounted when it comes to precision shooting cannot be overstressed; it is one of the essential foundations that precision shooting is built on, the other two being a properly set up rifle and a sound shooting technique. If any one of these three is missing, or even compromised in some way to the smallest degree, then precision shooting will be just a dream.

THE ZEROING PROCESS

If you are reading this book on advanced airgun hunting then you should already be a competent airgun shooter. Therefore you will already know how to zero in a scope correctly, but now you are broadening your skill level so that you can engage long-range live targets. You also have to make the zeroing process more precise by ensuring that the rifle is perfectly still and level and that there is not the slightest bit of perceptible wind.

The best place to zero a rifle is on an indoor range that is totally unaffected by wind, but very few airgun hunters have access to such a range. Using woodland or other natural features that block out the wind is also an effective way of making sure that the wind does not affect your zeroing. Having used the method above to bore sight your scope there should not need to be much, if any, adjustment made to the windage so, if you are making heavy adjustments you know that the wind is too strong for precise zeroing. To ensure that the rifle is perfectly still and level when zeroing use a shooting bench, or the bipod and shooting bag as explained previously.

The importance of keeping the rifle completely still and level during the zeroing process cannot be overstressed, as the very slightest movement will have an impact on the strike point. When carrying out normal airgun hunting, most shooters just zero the rifle in the prone position, supporting the rifle with the arms. However, if the rifle is set up to be self-supporting, and therefore perfectly still, then every shot taken will be true, whereas the shot taken by the shooter supporting the rifle with the arms is influenced by the shooter's wobble factor. Since wobble will vary considerably, the rifle zeroed in this manner is not zeroed true and will therefore offer variations in shot placement which, although small, will make the rifle incapable of true precision.

However the rifle that is set up to be self-supporting in a completely level position will, if extreme care is taken when squeezing the trigger during the zeroing process, be a rifle that has a true zero and is therefore capable of achieving extreme degrees of accuracy. A lot of shooters think that advanced long-range shooting has something to do with special shooting positions that magically improve accuracy. However, that is not the case at all; advanced hunting is founded on setting up the shooting rig correctly so that everything, from the scope to the trigger, is set to the highest possible standard of precision. The shooting positions used by the advanced hunter are the same as those used by the beginner and the intermediate hunter; the element that takes the shooting up to the advanced level is the ability to use the equipment to its optimum capacity.

THE CORRECT SCOPE AND AIMING GRID FOR LONG-RANGE SHOOTING AT LIVE QUARRY

I stated in Chapter One that in order to carry out long-range shots at live quarry the shooter needs to have the very best rifle available, a rifle capable of pushing the discipline of airgun hunting to its very limits. The same is true of the scope that you use on your rifle – any old scope just will not do – it has to be of the very best quality with a sophisticated aiming grid, top of the range lenses that present a crisp, well-defined image, an adjustable parallax and variable magnification. The adjustable parallax should be of the side-mounted variety, so that you can look through the scope and move the parallax wheel at the same time – something that is extremely difficult, if not impossible, to do when the parallax is set in the front of the scope as a rotating ring.

You may ask why it is necessary to be able to adjust the parallax and look through the scope at the same time, because the parallax on a really good quality scope can be used as a very effective and quick range-finding device. If the magnification is set at 10× you can look through the ocular lens and move the parallax wheel till the target you are looking at comes into sharp focus. Then simply look at the parallax wheel and see what range the dial is reading and you have the range to your target. You want a variable magnification for two reasons: firstly so that you can adjust the magnification setting to compensate for the different eye relief that occurs due to adopting different shooting positions and, secondly, so that you can adjust the magnification for daytime and night-time shooting activities.

the side-mounted
parallax wheel

The side-mounted parallax adjustment.

AIMING GRID

The aiming grid is the pattern used to form the reticle. I shall only be looking at aiming grids designed by Hawke scopes as they have the most sophisticated range of aiming grids available to the airgun hunter and, in fact, several of their scope designs are now being used in America by sharpshooters in the SWAT teams in numerous states. Professional shooters need the very best equipment available because a missed shot for them does not mean the loss of a rabbit, but the loss of a life, so the equipment they use has to be capable of delivering a first shot hit, each and every time. The fact that they are now using Hawke scopes is testament to the extreme accuracy that a Hawke top-end scope is capable of delivering. Let us take a look at some of the aiming grids that are used in Hawke scopes and see which one of them best suits the needs of the long-range airgun hunter.

30/30 Duplex

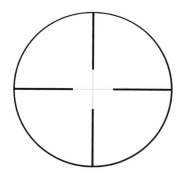

The 30/30 Duplex reticle.

The 30/30 Duplex is a very popular reticle pattern because it is simple to use and very effective. The narrowing of the posts to a very fine cross hair means that it does not obscure the target. The 30/30 Duplex can be used as a range-finding device, but this function is better suited to larger quarry such as deer, which are obviously beyond the capacity of the airgun hunter. The 30/30 Duplex offered by Hawke can be illuminated, as can most of the reticles that they offer, and I

shall consider the value of illumination later in this section. The 30/30 Duplex is a good, sound reticle, but it is not the best choice for the long-range airgun hunter because it does not offer a range of accurately spaced aim points, relying instead on the shooter's ability to estimate holds and leads; it also does not provide a sufficient degree of range-finding capability.

Illuminated L4 Dot

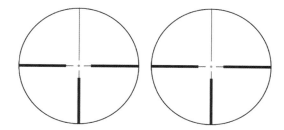

The illuminated dot 4 reticle.

This reticle is a variation on the 30/30 Duplex, having no thick post on the upper vertical cross hair and a dot at the centre of the grid, this variation allowing for a clearer view of the target. The thick posts on the horizontal cross hair are there to frame the target in dark brush, where the fine sections of the post will disappear. The centre dot illuminates so as to be viable in low light conditions. This aiming grid can be used for simple range-finding applications but not for the more precision range finding required by the long-range airgun hunter. The centre dot is very effective at engaging moving quarry, making this pattern an excellent choice for pest control operations on feral pigeon or rat.

MAP 6

The MAP 6 resembles a 30/30 Duplex but has aiming points arranged along the centre cross which are similar to, but not the same as, Mil Dots. The aim points on the Map 6 offer numerous options for hold over, hold under and windage leads. The aim points, unlike Mil Dots, are not equally

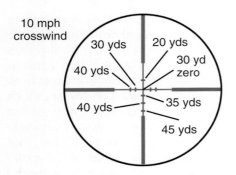

The MAP 6 reticle.

A small aim point Vs a large aim point.

spaced but set at junctures that relate to the trajectory of airgun ammunition. The centre cross is designed to be zeroed at 30yd, with the other aim points offering increments that relate to a shift in the strike point of 5yd. As an aiming grid for general purpose airgun hunting there is none better than the MAP 6, as this is the prime purpose for which the pattern was designed. However, as far as long-range, advanced hunting goes, there is not a sufficient degree of precision in the range-finding capacity of the MAP 6.

MAP 6A

The MAP 6A reticle.

The MAP 6A is a highly sophisticated aiming grid, designed to offer multiple aim points that calibrate to the trajectory of your rifle and a very accurate range-finding capacity. The aim points are not, in this case, dots, but lines with triangular ends. With such very fine aim points it is possible to achieve a very acute level of aim point placement allowing for a more precise delivery of the shot. In fact with such a fine aim point it is almost possible to split an atom.

As with the MAP 6, the MAP 6A is designed to be zeroed at 30yd, with the aim points offering a 5yd shift in the strike point. The range-finding ability of the MAP 6A involves bracketing a target with a known size along the aim points, or within the hollow portions of the posts below the aim points. The BRC (Ballistic Reticle Calculator) that can be freely downloaded from the Deben website, allows you to figure out what bracketing to use on a target of a known size at different ranges. There is really little point me going into the subject in any great detail as the website is packed with helpful information that explains how to utilize the range-finding capacity of the MAP 6A reticule to the full. The MAP 6A reticle is one of the best aiming grids available on the market today and is the perfect choice for the airgun hunter seeking to engage long-range targets. This reticle pattern is available in the Nite Eye range of scopes from Hawke, which, despite its name, is also a very effective scope for daytime shooting. It also offers some very special features for night-time hunting, which we shall look at later in the chapter on hunting in the dark.

SR6 IR

This again is a very sophisticated aiming grid and combined range-finding device; the designation for this scope, SR6, stands for Specialized Reticle 6 and it is designed to meet the needs of the shooter looking for extreme levels of accuracy. This is achieved by providing multiple aim points consisting of hollow dots that frame, rather than obscure, the strike point on the target. With this aim point you see more of the intended strike point than you will with any other kind of aim point – no matter how fine; the more clearly you can see the intended strike point the more precisely you can place the shot.

The windage aim points on the SR6 are unique because, rather than being spaced along the horizontal cross hair, as is the case on nearly all scopes, they are positioned on the vertical cross hair, arguably making for a more precise use of the windage aim points in mild winds. The windage aim points are calibrated to deal with winds up to 10mph; in winds stronger than this there are no windage aim points and, since I often shoot in winds of 20mph and will even venture out in gales, then, unfortunately, there are insufficient windage aim points to suit my

The laptop symbol means that the reticle is compatible with the Hawke Ballistic calculations program.

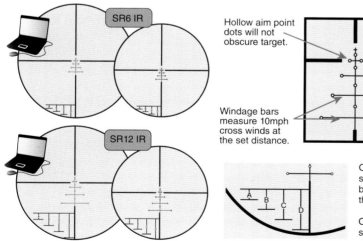

Hollow aim point dots will not obscure target.

Windage bars measure 10mph cross winds at the set distance.

SR (Specialized Reticles) © Hawke

The reticles have a series of hollow dots and crosses that are positioned on the vertical, at specific points, to suit the parabolic curve of a rifles trajectory.

Unlike Mil Dots and most other reticles, the aim points are not an equal distance apart. This favors the SR reticles as the calculated aim points are more evenly spaced. The windage bars, flanked by hollow dot windage aim points, represent 10mph side winds at their given distance.

On the bottom left of the Field of View is a range finding bracketing system, allowing the distance to a target to be calculated. Simply bracket the known size target, between A,B,C or D, then calculate the distance.

On 6× mag. - SR6 reticle and 12× mag. - SR12 reticle, range finding spacing measures A=3" B=6" C=9" D=12" at 50yds.

SR Reticles are registered designs, US Patent Nos. 29/230,616 European Registration Nos.000 262 795-001-004 © Hawke

The SR6 reticle.

needs. This is a shame as the SR6 offers one of the most precise aiming grids available and, if you live in an area where the wind is less savage, or you do most of your shooting in wooded areas where the effect of the wind is all but negated, then this pattern is well worth considering.

Unlike many other forms of aiming grid, the aim points do not have a dual role and therefore do not act as a range-finding device, this function being transferred to a descending series of spacing measures placed conveniently in the bottom left-hand quarter of the reticle. These spacing measures are used to measure the height of a target with a known measurement; the range is then discerned by the height the target reads on the spacing measure.

The BRC can be used to work out the range-finding specifics of the SR6, as well as enabling you to match trajectory to aim points, which of course saves many hours of experimenting on the range. I must admit that I still prefer to be on the range experimenting with the gun scope and ammunition rather than sitting at a computer, but in today's computer-controlled world that puts me in a distinct minority and there is no doubt that the BRC is a very effective and rapid tool for computing range-finding data and the matching of aim points to trajectory. The SR6 aiming grid is available in the Sidewinder range of scopes, which are considered to be among the very best scopes available on the market today.

Mil Dot

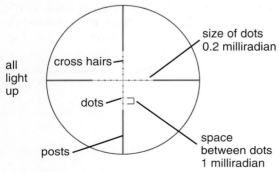

The Mil Dot reticle.

The mil dot needs little introduction as it is the standard pattern used on most scopes these days and, though still very popular among airgun shooters, it has really been surpassed by the much more sophisticated aiming grids that Hawke offers. Even though the dot is extremely small, one of the biggest drawbacks of the mil dot system, compared to the MAP 6A, the SR6 and other patterns from Hawke, is that next to the aim points from these aiming grids, the dot looks like a football and, consequently, is not the best choice for the precise placement of shoots on small targets.

A sniper working on human-sized targets at ranges of 1000yd will not find that the mil dot obscures the target, in fact at that kind of range a bolder mil dot is preferable, but at ranges below 50yd on small targets, such as the head of a rabbit, the finer the aim point, within reason, the better. So the mil dot for long-range hunting is somewhat outdated.

The range-finding capacity of the mil dot reticle has also been surpassed by five or six much more advanced aiming grids offered by Hawke Optics, so I will just make one final point which is that the 'mil' in mil dot does not stand for millimetre, as some shooters suppose, but milliradian, which is a very precise and somewhat complex form of measurement. The term 'mil dot' does not refer to the size of the dot, but to the space between the dots, so when the scope is referred to as a 'mil dot scope' it means that there is one milliradian of space between each dot. The dots themselves will measure much less than one milliradian, a common measurement for the dot being 0.2 milliradian. When we move on to the next aiming grid you will see the point of this explanation of the term mil dot spacing.

½ Mil Dot

On the mil dot aiming grid, the spacing between the dots is a milliradian. Unlike the mil dot aiming grid, the dots on the ½ mil dot reticle are not too large for very precise placement on small targets. In fact the dots on the ½ mil dot are extremely fine indeed,

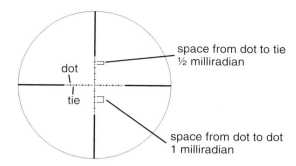

The ½ Mil Dot reticle.

presenting negligible obstruction of the kill zone. However, the real beauty in this system lies in the spacing between the dots which has been cut down to ½ a milliradian, so there are double the number of aim points, allowing for extreme precision because a greater number of ranges are covered by the larger number of dots.

For example, on a standard mil dot scope you would, if zeroed at 30yd when tackling a target at 32yd, have to move down the vertical cross hair to the 35yd aim point. However, on a ½ mil dot scope there is an aim point between 30 and 35yd that will be 32 ½ yd. The ½ mil dot grid then provides for a much more accurate placement of the pellet in the kill zone, enhancing the precision, not because the shooter is any better, but because the aiming grid he is using gives him a greater level of aim point selection.

Much of the long-range hunting equipment improves the shooter's abilities, although a deep understanding of how to use the equipment must also be present, along with a sound basic shooting technique. Whilst a very good shot will be able to achieve respectable results with nothing more than a standard cross hair, their shot placement radically improves when the more sophisticated aiming grids are employed.

The ½ mil dot aiming grid is also a very precise tool for range finding a target of a known size, which can be bracketed between the dots to ascertain its range. The Deben BRC programme can be used to work out with great precision the correlation between

the range to the target and its bracketing between the dots. Just as the number of dots increases on the vertical cross hair, so they also increase on the horizontal cross hair, providing a vast range of aim points for windage corrections to be made – even sufficient for me on my windy Scottish hunting grounds. This is an excellent reticle for those looking to engage in advanced long-range hunting with an air rifle and it appears in the Varmint range of specialist long-range hunting scopes.

This is a great choice for the airgun hunter who wants to take his shots out to long range but cannot quite afford the more sophisticated reticles found in a Sidewinder scope, which cost roughly £300. The Varmint, with a 3-12×44 configuration on the other hand, comes in at about £130, and that includes a side-mounted, adjustable parallax. This is an essential feature on a scope intended for long range as it allows you to gain the clearest sight, easily and rapidly, by dialling in a range setting to correspond with the range to the target. The parallax ring can also be used as a range-finding device if required. If you are looking for exceptional value for money then the Varmint scope is unbeatable in every respect.

10× and 20× ½ Mil Dot

Now we come to the ultimate in reticles, the 10× and 20× ½ mil dot pattern, designed by Hawke Optics, which is among the most sophisticated reticles in the world. It is designed for the shooter seeking extremely acute levels of shot placement; whether that is an airgun hunter seeking to take down a rabbit at the very edge of a weapon's capabilities, or a SWAT marksman aiming to neutralize the threat being posed by an armed gunman (this is the reticle that is now in service with numerous police departments in the USA, which gives you an idea of how highly it is regarded).

The reticle is a combination of a precision aiming grid of the ½ mil dot type mentioned above, and a very accurate range-finding device in the form of hollow posts divided

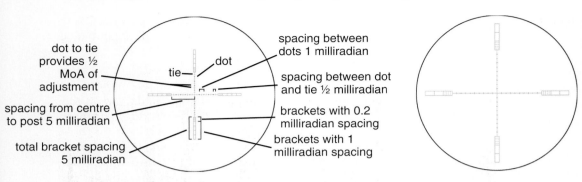

dot to tie provides ½ MoA of adjustment

tie

dot

spacing between dots 1 milliradian

spacing between dot and tie ½ milliradian

spacing from centre to post 5 milliradian

brackets with 0.2 milliradian spacing

total bracket spacing 5 milliradian

brackets with 1 milliradian spacing

The 10x ½ Mil Dot reticle.

The 20x ½ Mil Dot reticle.

The 20x ½ Mil Dot Sidewinder with 30mm tube.

The focus adjustment ring.

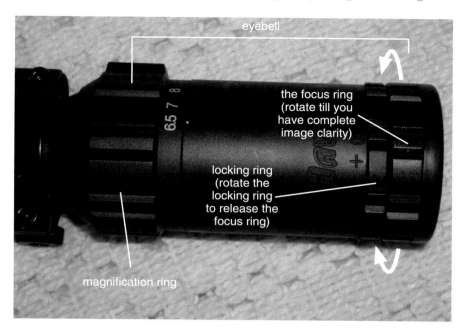

eyebell

the focus ring (rotate till you have complete image clarity)

locking ring (rotate the locking ring to release the focus ring)

magnification ring

elevation turret

windage turret

The windage and elevation turrets.

to unlock the
turret so that
compensation
coordinates can be
dialled in, lift it up

The turret unlocked.

To reset the turret scale to 0 loosen this screw. Change turret, and retighten.

the side-mounted parallax wheel

The parallax wheel.

into brackets. The first portion of this bracketing containing five brackets with 0.2 milliradian spacing makes them ideal for the range finding of small targets like the rabbit. The fact that the bracketing in the upper portion of the post is divided into so many segments means that, using it in conjunction with the larger brackets beneath, you can achieve a very precise range. The reason for this is the fact that there are so many measuring markers with the bracketing system and the more markers there are, the more precise the measurement you can make.

If you have a ruler marked only in inches then all you can do is measure in increments of an inch, but if the ruler were divided into ½ and ¼ inches, then you could make measurements in increments of a fraction. The bracketing system on the 10× and 20× ½ mil dot reticle is like the ruler marked with fractions; it provides smaller increments and therefore more accurate range finding which, of course, means a more accurate placement of the shot within the kill zone.

The precision of this reticle does not just lie within the range-finding facility but in the aiming grid that offers ½ MOA between aim points; that is ½ Minute Of Angle, which is ½ an inch at 100yd, or 1cm at 100yd. All that means is that when you move from one aim point to another at 100yd, the shift in the strike point is a very fine 1cm or 10mm. As airgun hunters, even at long range we are not going to be tackling targets at such a range, but all that you need to do in order to bring the above calculation down to the range of 40yd is divide 1cm by 100 (this being the 100yd) which gives us 0.01, and then times that by 40 (this being 40yd) which calculates at 0.4cm which is 4mm.

From all this we know that when shooting at ranges of 40yd, when you move from one aim point to another the shift in the strike point will be an incredible 4mm. You should now be able to see that this aiming grid is capable of very precise shot placements and extremely fine adjustments. All well-made reticles are precise tools, but this one takes

precision to the very extreme and, in my opinion, is the finest aiming grid that you can put on your air rifle.

SWAT teams now using the 10× and 20× ½ mil dot reticle previously employed scopes costing thousands of pounds, but the extreme precision they can achieve with the 10× and 20× ½ mil dot pattern has persuaded them to move away from the vastly more expensive scopes which did not offer the same facility.

I should offer some explanation as to what is meant by 10× and 20× ½ mil dot. It simply means that the 10× reticle is true to all the specified milliradian spacings, when the scope is set on 10× magnification. At other magnifications, the spacings are not true and so for range finding the scope needs to be used on the 10× magnification setting. If you require more or less magnification to make the shot simply dial in the preferred magnification after range-finding. Shifting the magnification should not alter the aim points but it will alter the eye relief on some scopes by as much as ½ an inch.

The eye relief becomes less as you increase the magnification so, on such scopes, it is necessary to alter your stock weld accordingly. If you don't do this you will have a shift in the strike point which, in turn, will cause a miss that you will find hard to understand if you are not aware of the shifting eye relief issue.

The 20× ½ mil dot reticle obviously offers true spacing when set at 20×, which is the magnification you will have to select for range finding, but such a high magnification is too high for taking the shot; radically reducing the field of view 10× to 12× magnification is the preferred high magnification option that offers a much deeper field of view. You need to have the larger field of view because targets such as rabbits will not oblige and stay still whilst you line up the perfect shot. It is quite often the case that when the cross hairs are locked on the kill zone the rabbit will move and, in order to maintain visual contact with the target, you need a wide field of view. A narrow field of view will mean the loss of the target, requiring you to move the rifle to re-establish contact with the target. However, such a movement can betray your position, whereas the shooter with a deeper field of view will only have to make the very slightest adjustment to regain the target.

The point being that you need to use the 20× magnification to get a pinpoint accurate range, but then you need to reduce that magnification down to 10× to make the shot. On the subject of the field of view, you will find that manufacturers offer figures for the field of view that a particular scope offers. The figure is generally given in feet at a range of 100yd, there being two figures, the first for the lowest magnification and the second for the highest magnification that the scope offers. For example the 10× ½ mil dot reticle with a variable magnification from 4.5× to 14× with a 42mm objective lens has a field of view at 100yd of 23–6.9ft. So at 4.5× magnification the field of view (FOV) is 23ft, so you will see 23ft of ground through the ocular lens at 100yd, and when the magnification goes up to 14× the FOV shrinks dramatically down to 6.9ft. For long-range airgun hunting you want to select a scope that has an FOV where the first figure given is preferably 20ft or more, and certainly no less than 16ft.

So now we come to the scope in which the 10× and 20× ½ mil dot reticle is used: the superlative Sidewinder Tactile, a masterpiece of the scope manufacturer's art with a worldwide reputation. The scope offers a very strong 30mm tube that can take an incredible amount of abuse – even really severe blows do not damage it – nor do they shift the zero, which is a definite plus point because there are plenty of scopes on the market that, if they take even the slightest tap, suffer a zero shift.

Because a 30mm tube is used you not only get strength but also a greater degree of adjustment in the windage and elevation turrets, simply because there is more room within the tube for adjustments to take place. A 30mm tube also draws more light than a 1in tube, but the fact is that the quality of the light coming through a scope is not to do with the size of the tube, but the size of the exit pupil and the quality of the lenses. The lenses used in the Sidewinder Tactical are fully multi-coated, high quality lenses offering an exit pupil of sufficient size to meet the eye's optimum light requirement. In turn this means a crystal clear image, which is an obvious essential for precise shot placement.

The reticle is glass etched, which means that the aiming grid is etched onto a piece of glass and, because of the room within the 30mm tube, robust springs are fitted to move the reticle, making for very sure movements. The sound of the movements when you turn the turrets resembles the sound you get when you wind an old Swiss pocket watch and is the sound of a quality internal mechanism. There are 305 clicks in the windage turret and 298 clicks in the elevation turret so, when the turrets are rotated to the end of their scale, 152 windage and 149 elevation clicks will centre the cross hairs, aligning the centre of the aiming grid with the centre of the exit pupil.

The turrets on the Sidewinder are of the push/pull, locking variety so when the turret is pulled up it is in the unlocked position and may be rotated to effect click movement on the reticle. When the turret is pushed down it locks in place, preventing accidental movement of the turret. Both turrets have a scale on them, the elevation turret being marked from zero to fourteen and the windage turret being marked zero to seven for right-hand movement, and zero to seven for left-hand movement. The scale on these turrets can be reset, which means that once you have zeroed the rifle you can use a star key to loosen the screw in the top of the turret. This will allow you to rotate the scale on the turret without affecting a click on the reticle in order to align the zero on both scales, with the mark on the base of the turret, the screw in both turrets is then tightened.

Resetting the turrets in this manner means that adjustments can be made to the windage and elevation and the zero recovered by turning the scale back to zero.

Instead of using the off-set aiming points to engage targets at ranges that are not at zero, the shooter can dial in coordinates that have been calculated on the range so that the centre cross is re-zeroed to engage the target. This is the technique used by snipers and is the most precise use of the aiming grid because the centre cross is superior to the other aim points for alignment on the kill zone, especially if corrections have to be made for windage.

So why bother with multiple aim points? The simple answer is that they offer a rapid mode or target acquisition, which is sometimes required when the target animal is only available to be shot for a few seconds. This would not give sufficient time for turret adjustment but, when there is time for turret adjustment, a finer placement of the shot is possible. To find out what adjustments have to dialled into the turrets for differing ranges and wind speeds, you will have to go

to the range and spend hours shooting your rifle to figure it all out – there is no computer programme to do this job for you.

With the scope zeroed at 30yd you want to set up targets at 32, 35, 37 and 40yd, then shoot at all these targets; re-zero the rifle and note down the coordinate on the elevation turret (this first session should be done on a day when there is no wind, so there should not need to be any adjustment to the windage turret). Return to the zero mark for each new range; do not, for example, zero the rifle for 32yd, write down the coordinate, then zero at 35yd, without returning to the zero mark. The reason for this is that you need to go from zero directly to the required range when engaging a target; you do not want to work through the ranges in graduated stages.

When you have got a complete record for the longer distances, do the same for the shorter distances, these being: 28yd, 25yd, 23yd and 20yd. Very rarely will you need a zero lower than 20yd, but for pest control of rat and feral pigeon then lower zeros will be required. For such work you will need a different scope, the Sidewinder being designed for the long-range engagement of targets. To discover the coordinate that you will need to dial in for windage adjustment, known as 'hold off', then you will have to visit the range on numerous separate occasions, in different wind speeds from a still day up to about 25mph.

I live in a very windy environment and, although some airgun hunters will tell you that it is impossible to hunt in winds above 20mph with an airgun they are wrong; I have hunted in gale-strength winds and taken very considerable bags by utilizing techniques I have developed for coping with the wind. But most shooters will only need to calculate for wind speeds up to 25mph. You will then need to have coordinates for the following wind speeds: calm 1mph, slight air movement 3mph, light breeze 3–5mph, gentle

Wind Speed in MPH									
		3	3–5	5–8	8–12	12–16	16–20	20–25	
Range in Yards	Elevation Adjustment	Windage Adjustment							
20									
23									
25									
28									
30	0								
32									
35									
37									
40									

breeze 5–8mph, moderate breeze 8–12mph, fresh breeze 12–16mph, strong breeze 16–20mph, near gale 20–25mph.

You will need to go through the entire selection of ranges to which you have a zero coordinate, at all the wind speeds stipulated above. Nobody will be able to remember all the coordinates involved with all these ranges and wind speeds, but a simple chart can be made up to record all the information that can be taped to the sunshade of your scope for easy reference.

Zero Record Card

You can now see why so few shooters go to the trouble of dialling in turret coordinates for different ranges and wind speeds, due to the large amount of work involved in order to build up a chart of coordinates. However, if you wish to become an advanced airgun hunter then you have to put in the work so the hunter wishing to become an advanced hunter must put in a significant level of complex work to achieve the goal of the deadly precision placement of a projectile at long range on the very small kill zone of the target quarry. You may still doubt that

dialling in turret coordinates offers a more precise alignment of the aim point but the following diagram should help to convince you of the fact.

The Sidewinder Tactical with 30mm tube has a side-, as opposed to a front-mounted, parallax adjustment, the advantage being that when you are in the prone shooting position, with the front of the rifle well supported by the bipod, you can easily reach forward and manipulate the parallax wheel with the minimum of movement so as not to attract the attention of your quarry. The front-mounted parallax ring, on the other hand, is very hard to manipulate when in the shooting position; it also requires a more extended movement that is much more likely to attract the eye of your quarry.

The parallax adjustment on the Sidewinder is operated by a wheel, which, due to its size, makes the movement of the parallax a smooth and easy affair. You will see some scopes that have a huge side wheel to turn the parallax and, whilst this is fine on the range for target shooting, in the field such a huge wheel is easily snagged or entangled with the undergrowth in the prone position. This is why the Sidewinder has a much more

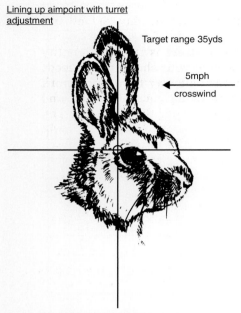

Lining up aimpoint with turret adjustment

Target range 35yds

5mph crosswind

Making turret adjustments means that the centre of the crosshairs can be used to precisely place the aimpoint directly on the required strike point so there is no element of estimation.

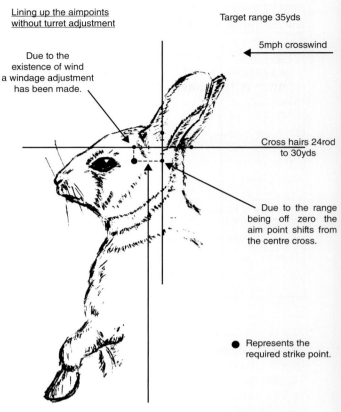

Lining up the aimpoints without turret adjustment

Target range 35yds

5mph crosswind

Due to the existence of wind a windage adjustment has been made.

Cross hairs 24rod to 30yds

Due to the range being off zero the aim point shifts from the centre cross.

● Represents the required strike point.

When windage and elevation adjustments are applied the windage and elevation aim points have to be aligned on the required strike point and no matter how well this is done there is always a degree of estimation.

The advantage of dialling in range coordinates.

conservatively sized wheel. It is attention to detail like this that makes the difference between a scope that is brilliant in the field and one that, despite all its promise, is a nightmare to use.

The very accurate adjustable parallax on the Sidewinder is one of the most valuable features of this scope as it is a precise range-finding vehicle. Simply place the 10× ½ Mil Dot Sidewinder on 10× magnification with the parallax set on its lowest setting of 10yd then, looking through the scope, observe the target quarry and rotate the parallax wheel until the target presents a clear image in the ocular lens. When this happens, read off the range that the paral-

lax is set on and you have the range from the scope to the target.

Using the parallax for range finding is my preferred method; however, it is only possible if the rifle is supported, such as on a bipod. With unsupported firing positions you need both hands to hold the rifle and therefore cannot manipulate the parallax wheel or dial coordinates into the turrets. This is one of the reasons why the long-range airgun hunter should always have the rifle supported to take a shot; the other reason being that a supported rifle is infinitely more accurate than one supported by the body alone.

With the 20× ½ Mil Dot Sidewinder with 30mm tube, you will need to set the scope on 20× magnification to use the parallax for range finding. To facilitate the reading of the scale on the parallax wheel, a pointer is mounted to the body tube; the reading on the parallax wheel that is in line with the pointer is the range at which the parallax is set.

One small quibble I have is that the markings on the parallax wheel of the Sidewinder are marked with very fine white lines and numbering that is not easy to identify in dull conditions, or when hunting at night. The pointer tip, which functions as the reader, is also matt black and in dull conditions or when night hunting it is invisible. The situation is easily remedied by taking a modeller's paint brush and applying white paint to the pointer, enabling it to be seen in all conditions; if you can get your hands on some fluorescent paint then even better. As to the markings on the parallax wheel, I have also used the modeller's paintbrush on them, turning the skinny lines into broad ones that can be easily seen.

Making improvements like this to your equipment is one of the features of advanced airgun hunting. A lot of shooters do not want to ruin the look of a piece of equipment but what matters is its functionality so, if some piece of your shooting rig needs to be altered in some way to make it work better, thus improving your efficiency and accuracy, then carry out the alteration and never mind what it looks like. You should not be thinking of the resale value of the rifle or other pieces of equipment, all that should concern you is how well the items work. Guns and scopes are tools; they are not fashion accessories.

One other little quibble I have with the Sidewinder scopes is that the parallax range markings go from 15yd to 25yd to 50yd. I would prefer 25yd, 30yd, 35yd and 40yd, making the parallax a much more versatile range-finding vehicle. You can, however, with practice learn to use the parallax to read the 30yd, 35yd and 40yd ranges.

The Sidewinder comes with a sunshade that screws into the front of the scope and, as the name suggests, its prime function is to

Enhanced scope markings.

prevent too much sun getting into the scope, which would cause a whiteout. However, I fit the sunshade to the scope every time I go out hunting for a number of reasons, not just to prevent excessive amounts of sun getting down the scope. The sunshade also protects the objective lens from damage, especially when working in thick brush. In the rain it helps to keep water off the objective lens, especially when operating in windy conditions. Another service that the sun shade provides when night hunting is to protect the objective lens from the glare of the scope-mounted light, which I like to have mounted very close to the objective lens which would not be possible unless the sunshade was fitted.

Both the 10× and 20× ½ Mil Dot Sidewinder scopes in a 30mm tube are fitted with a multi-illuminating reticle that can be illuminated in red and green. The red is for working on targets in dull or dark conditions and the green for the acquisition of targets in daylight conditions. I would prefer a blue illumination for daytime work, which is the more effective form of illumination for daytime shooting, but green is still a highly effective colour for the engagement of target quarry.

I am generally against illuminated reticles as the illumination turns the fine cross hairs and dots on the mil dot into great posts, with football-sized dots that completely obscure the kill zone, destroying any hope of seriously precise shot placement. On most scopes with an illuminated reticle I normally leave the battery out and never use the illumination facility, however, I make an exception for the Sidewinder as the illumination does not swell the cross hairs or mil dots at all, and the red illumination for contrast against the kill zone of quarry during night hunting expeditions is a very effective tool that does improve reticle alignment and thus shot placement.

However, I do not really see the value of an illumination for daytime conditions, when the straight black cross hairs and black mil dots are my preferred option. However, when rabbits are beneath overhanging trees, or when the light begins to fade, or on days darkened by heavy cloud, the green illumination is of some value, presenting a vivid contrast against the kill zone.

The illumination of both green and red is graduated in stages of brightness from one to five, but I generally find that I never operate the illumination on lower than the three setting, one and two being superfluous in my opinion. One complaint I have about the dial that operates the illumination is that it is too small and stiff and requires much bigger lugs to facilitate easy operation. I intend to make some kind of wheel that will fit over the illumination adjuster and clamp it so that I am able to operate the illumination function with a much greater degree of ease. Despite the few minor quibbles I have the Sidewinder scope is, nevertheless, one of the best scopes in the world today for long-range airgun hunting applications.

Chapter 3
The Chronograph and a Few Words About Pellets

CHAPTER OBJECTIVES:

Knowledge:

From this chapter you will learn what a chronograph is and gain a knowledge of why it is necessary to use a chronograph to observe the power output of your rifle. You will also have a clear understanding of what kind of pellet is best suited to long-range hunting applications.

Practical Skills:

By the end of this chapter you will be able to set up and operate a chronograph and be proficient in interpreting the data it provides. You will also be able to prepare pellets for long-range shooting.

Time Period Required To Gain Practical Skills:

Two to four hours.

THE CHRONOGRAPH AND HOW TO USE IT

A chronograph is a device that measures the speed of a moving object, generally in fps (feet per second), by timing its speed of travel between two sets of sensors, mounted one at the front and the other at the rear of the chronograph machine. A chronograph is a very complex piece of equipment and there is no need to have an in-depth understanding of how it works; simply recognizing that it has the ability to measure the velocity

of a pellet fired from an air rifle in fps is sufficient.

So why do we need to use a chronograph? The answer is to acquaint ourselves with the ballistic character of the rifle we are using, in terms of power output. From this simple piece of information we can determine what the rifle is capable of achieving and the health of the weapon's power output. If the power output drops or rises, even by small degrees, that has an effect on the projectile, altering its flight path and strike point. The shift in the strike point may be extremely small (and many shooters would call it insignificant), but if extreme precision is your goal then a shift in strike point, no matter how small, is a shift nonetheless and should be corrected.

In extremely cold weather, a common occurrence in the part of Scotland where I live, but by no means unfamiliar to other parts of the British Isles, there is a significant effect on the power output of your rifle. If your rifle has been factory set, as many rifles are, at 11.2 to 11.5ft/lb, and the cold weather reduces your power output by .5ft/lb, you could find yourself shooting a rifle that is offering as little as 10.7ft/lb, which is going to reduce the range at which you can achieve an effective kill.

This is something that you need to be aware of before you set out on the hunt; it is not acceptable to take the shot then suddenly start to question why your rifle is not killing quarry, but injuring it. It is not uncommon to see in airgun magazines, letters written by shooters stating that the rifle they are using, which used to be an effective killing weapon, is no longer

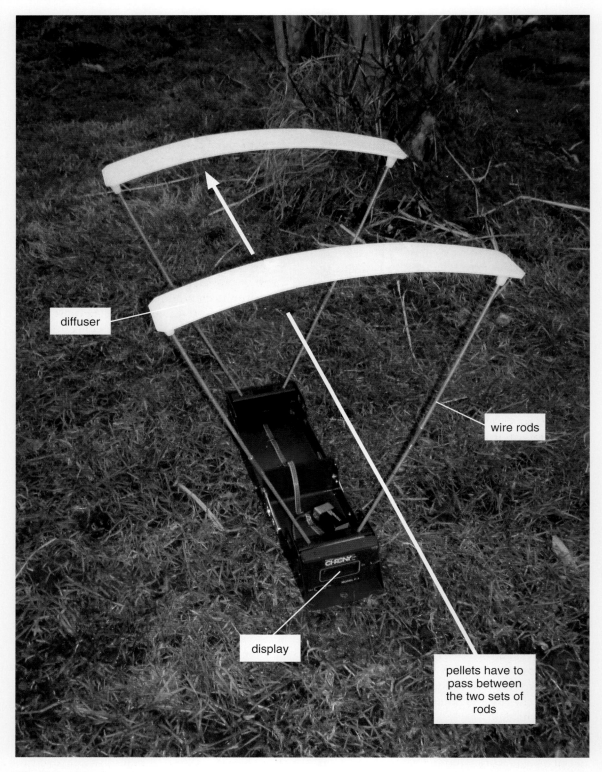

diffuser

wire rods

display

pellets have to pass between the two sets of rods

The chronograph.

killing the target quarry. The way they are discovering this fact is by shooting at animals, not killing them, and leaving them injured, which is completely unacceptable and totally avoidable if a chronograph is used before every hunting expedition.

A chronograph is not something that an airgun hunter *should* own; it is something that they *must* own, especially if they intend to engage in long-range shots at live quarry. For the shooter working at ranges not exceeding 30yd, a barrel-mounted chronograph is sufficient and will calculate what power output the rifle is producing. For advanced airgun hunting however, you will need a free-standing chronograph that can be set up at the muzzle, and at various other ranges right out to 40yd, so that you can calculate the power output of your rifle at every range from 10yd to 40yd.

This is vital for long-range hunting, as you have to know if the rifle you are using is imparting sufficient power to the pellet to kill at the extended ranges of advanced airgun shooting. It takes approximately 4ft/lb of power in the projectile to kill a rabbit cleanly, so your rifle needs to be discharging pellets that are holding at least 6ft/lb at 40yd, but preferably 8ft/lb, for the rifle to be effective at long range. You may think that if it only takes 4ft/lb to kill the rabbit, why do you need the projectile at 40yd to be carrying more than 4ft/lb? The answer is because you need to have a comfortable margin of overkill of 1.5 to 2 times the required killing power, to ensure that the job is done cleanly and effectively.

4ft/lb is the base figure, the minimum amount of power required to bring about a kill; it is not, however, the optimum strike power, 8ft/lb producing a much deeper and more devastating wound tract. The more power you can deliver to the brain of the animal or bird with the pellet, the more catastrophic the injury, the surer the kill and the quicker the death.

The only way to discover if your rifle is producing sufficient power for long-range shooting is not to go out and see if you can kill rabbits at the 40yd range, but to fire a string of pellets through a chronograph set up 40yd away from the rifle; this will tell you exactly what the rifle is capable of. Developing a detailed understanding of your rifle's character is key to the mastery of long-range shooting.

There are plenty of chronographs on the market that cost well in excess of £100, but they are not necessary. I use an F-1 Chrony from Uttings which costs only £80 and is a superb and easy to use piece of equipment. This chronograph comes in the form of a metal box that opens out to reveal the light sensors and digital readout. Although I stated that you do not have to know all the ins and outs of how the chronograph works, it is useful to know that a light sensor at the front of the chronograph activates the electronic counter, which counts the speed of the pellet. The counter is then turned off by the light sensor in the rear of the chronograph, sensing the shadow of the pellet as is passes over the sensor.

The sensors are built into the top of the chronograph; they are not the metal rods that stick up out of the top of the chronograph (quite a few shooters make the mistake of thinking that the rods are the sensors). The rods coming from the top of the chronograph are simply a guide, designed to present a framed area to the shooter, in order to help them place their shot. In order for the light sensors to function there needs to be a cloudy sky. On bright sunny days with a blue sky the sensors will not function and so, on such days, diffusers have to be attached to the top of the alignment rods to simulate the effect of cloud cover.

I shall not go into the mechanics of setting up the chronograph here, as the instructions that come with it are very straightforward. It is simply a matter of opening up the chronograph, attaching a battery, placing the alignment rods into their respective holes and positioning the chronograph at the desired range and switching it on. The chronograph will need to sit on an object, such as a wooden box, to raise it up off the ground. You should also position a piece of wood (too thick for a pellet to penetrate) or a piece of

The digital display screen.

metal across the lower portion of the chronograph that houses the digital display and computer, otherwise, if a pellet strikes this area of the chronograph it will be destroyed as it is not pellet-proof.

The chronograph should be set up at various, precisely measured, ranges from the rifle: starting at the muzzle, then 10yd, 20yd, 30yd and finally 40yd. At each range you need to fire a string of at least fifteen shots to ascertain the power output of the rifle. Not every shot will produce exactly the same velocity or power output, there will be a variety and with a string of shots you will be able to see the top end and the low end of the variation.

Using this information you can then work out the rifle's variance: to calculate the variance you simply deduct the lowest fps reading from the highest in the string of fifteen shots. For rifles intended to carry out long-range shooting you need to see a variance of between four and seven fps, any higher than this and the rifle is not suitable for the field of advanced precision shooting.

The variance can change from one make of pellets to another, which is why it is important to try out your rifle with a wide selection of pellets, fired over the chronograph, to find out which pellets produce the lowest variance and the highest power output. The lower the variance, the closer the shots will be to one another on the target, but power is the most important feature; even so the variance must not be greater than seven fps. The variance in fps tells us about the velocity, or the speed at which the pellet travels from muzzle to target, but there is also another variance: the ft/lb variance or power variance.

Once all the shots in the string fired over the chronograph have been converted into ft/lb to give a power output reading, then you can deduct the lowest power output from the highest and end up with a power variance in ft/lb. For the purposes of long-range shooting, you do not want to be seeing a power variance of more than .2 or .3ft/lb. Make a record of the highest and lowest power outputs at all the specified ranges from muzzle to 40yd, then, before each hunting expedition, send a string of pellets over the chronograph at muzzle and 40yd range, to see if the power output has altered from that recorded.

Serious drops could mean that the rifle is defective in some way, or that you have simply neglected to recharge the air reservoir. You need to be having the same range of readings that you had when you zeroed the rifle. If you are getting readings of .5ft/lb above or below your top end and low end recorded chronograph readings from when the rifle was zeroed, then it may well be necessary to reset the zero.

The problem here is that, not only will you lose the zero at which the rifle has been set, but all the zero readings that you have recorded for other ranges. The coordinates dialled into the turrets will also have shifted, due to the change in power output, requiring you to make up a new zero record chart, which is not possible to do every time you want to go hunting.

Target shooters have the facility on their rifle to adjust the power output, by changing the tension on the hammer spring, allowing them to keep the rifle's power at a constant level and thus ensure that the power and zero remain in symmetry. Hunting rifles, unfortunately, do not offer this facility and if you remove the anti-tamper cap that covers the hammer spring adjuster, you void the warranty for your rifle. I, however, have removed the anti-tamper cap from my Theoben Tactical and regularly make small adjustments to the amount of tension on the hammer spring. This ensures that the rifle is producing exactly the same amount of power each time I use it and takes up the power slightly in cold weather.

I can also make adjustments to coordinate with the kind of pellets I am using, and reduce the power output for close range work where I want to avoid the problem of over-penetration. The internet is full of instructional material on how to increase the power output of a PCP, much of the material is from private individuals who are not trained gunsmiths, which is why some of the advice they put forward is of a dubious nature. You should avoid attempts at trying to take the power of your rifle up, the legal non-FAC limit is 12ft/lb and the hammer springs on most rifles will not allow you to go much above that anyway.

Tinkering with the regulator to get it to release more air per discharge, though advocated by some as a way of increasing the rifle's power, is not a sound idea as it can upset the smooth working of a rifle that has been calibrated so that everything works together; altering the regulator in isolation is, therefore, not a good idea. The only justifiable reason to want to make adjustments to the hammer spring is not to exceed the legal power output, but to allow you to make precise alterations to the power output; as target shooters do in order to maintain a consistent output and shot to shot accuracy.

The chronograph records the velocity of the pellet travelling across the sensors in

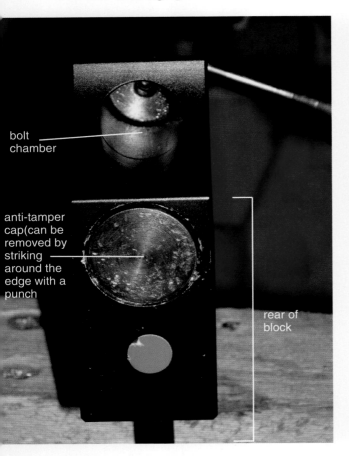

bolt
chamber

anti-tamper
cap(can be
removed by
striking
around the
edge with a
punch

rear of
block

turn in to
increase
power

turn out
decreas
power

hammer spring tension
adjuster

The anti-tamper cap located in the rear of the block.

With the anti-tamper cap removed the hammer spring adjuster is revealed (label).

fps, and you need to work out the power variance in ft/lb so, in order to do this, you need to use the conversion formula for turning velocity into power. The formula works on the average velocity of the string of shots fired over the chronograph, however, I always take the lowest velocity recorded over the string to make my calculation.

Formula:
Lowest velocity × Lowest velocity × Weight of pellet (in grains) divided by 450,240 = _____ ft/lb

Unless you happen to be a maths genius, add a cheap calculator to your shooting equipment in order to carry out quick calculations in the field when working with the chronograph.

PELLETS

Rather than go into pellet types and makes in this short discourse, I simply want to make a few points that the long-range hunter should be aware of. The first point is that, one of the rather brutal objectives of clean and effective hunting is to deliver a devastating wound to the brain of the target quarry. In order for that to happen, you need the heaviest pellet that your rifle can manage to propel out to 40yd, which will distort more effectively and carry less velocity than a lighter pellet and, therefore, it will impart more shock at the point of impact.

Today's obsession with lightweight, higher velocity air rifle pellets is not one that I share; I want the biggest, heaviest projectile that my rifle can accurately deliver, with a good sixty five per cent of its muzzle energy still being present at the strike point at a range of 40yd. Therefore, for long-range shooting, use the biggest, heaviest pellet that your rifle likes to shoot. This is something that you will have to find out for yourself; every single gun – even two guns from the same batch – has its own character, which is best suited to a particular pellet. When you get a new gun, try it with as many different quality pellets as you can get hold of, testing not just for accuracy on targets from 25 to 40yd, but testing over the chronograph to ascertain velocity and power variances.

A question that often gets asked is whether to weigh pellets. The weighing of pellets used to be very important, because the weight of pellets in a tin could vary quite considerably from one to another. However, pellet manufacture has come a very long way, and the variance between the heaviest and the lightest pellet to be found in a tin is now so small that it has no effect on the strike point of the pellet. However, there are many target shooters who still swear by the practise of weighing the pellets they shoot, working on the theory that, even in a good quality tin of pellets, there can be lurking a rogue or two that would strike well off the intended mark.

Pellets are also produced in batches, the batch number being printed somewhere on the tin with good-quality pellets. Whilst all the pellets in one batch may share uniformity in weight, another batch could vary very slightly, due to minute differences in the metal used to produce that batch. This is why target shooters buy their pellets in very large quantities, all from the same batch, a practise that I follow, buying my pellets 5000 at a time.

When you have pellets from a new batch

it is necessary to check that your zero is still sound, as well as checking the power output over the chronograph to see if the new batch is exhibiting any difference in strike point or power output. Scales for weighing pellets cost just over £20 so, if you want to weigh the pellets you use it will certainly do no harm and will lead to the discovery of any rogues. One Theoben rifle shooter told me that by weighing the pellets he used, he reduced the rifle's variance from 7fps down to 4fps, which would suggest that the weighing of pellets is of value and, since it takes so little time, you really have nothing to lose.

Target shooters also size the pellets that they use to make sure that they are of a uniform shape, a practice that seems to improve accuracy, although the sizing devices used are only manufactured for the target shooter who, for the obvious reason of trajectory, selects a .177 weapon. Hence all the sizing tools that I have come across are in .177 and most certainly not in my favourite calibre of .25. You can, however, use an engine's digital calibre to measure the head and the skirt of each pellet. This is a fairly tedious task, but it will allow you to eliminate any misshapen or undersized pellets, which is where the variance seems to occur. Pellets, no matter what they are made of, are fairly pliable and they can become easily deformed during manufacture or packing, so measuring them is a worthwhile exercise to ensure that every one going into the breech is of a uniform size and will, therefore, exhibit a uniform trajectory and maintain a consistent accurate strike point.

The washing of pellets is another practice favoured by target shooters and one that appears to increase the accuracy of the pellets. Although the improvement in accuracy between a washed pellet and an unwashed pellet is very small, when hunting at long range, small improvements in accuracy are well worth having as they can increase the precision with which the shot is placed, thus ensuring a first shot kill.

It is also true that when you make a very small improvement in accuracy in one area, the effect is multiplied because you are also making small improvements in several other areas. Any improvement in accuracy is therefore not going to work in isolation, but as part of the overall fine-tuning process that underpins advanced airgun hunting. When you wash your pellets, simply use some warm water and a drop or two of washing-up liquid and I am sure you will be surprised how much debris ends up in the bottom of the bowl. Remove the pellets one by one from the bowl and place them on kitchen towel to drain, then give them a blast with a hair dryer to ensure that they are fully dry and, once you are fully satisfied, store them away in a pellet pouch ready for use.

Before storing the pellets, you could give them a drop or two of pellet lube which, for reasons not clearly understood, increases the accuracy and the power of the pellet. To apply the pellet lube, place 100 pellets in a plastic freezer bag, then apply a few drops of lube; less is definitely more when it comes to pellets lube – overdo it and there will be a detrimental effect on pellet performance. Agitate the pellets in the plastic bag gently so that they all receive an even, fine coating of oil, and then place them in your pellet pouch.

Paying such close attention to the preparation of pellets may seem like a dull affair, but look at it as a way of enhancing the performance and effectiveness of your rifle. It is just like the firearms shooters who make their own loads, or the musket shooters who make their own shot. It is just such tiny attention to the smallest details that is going to take your shooting up to the next level.

Chapter 4
Night Vision Scopes and Other Equipment for Hunting at Night and in Dull Light

CHAPTER OBJECTIVES:

Knowledge:

By the end of this chapter you will have the knowledge required to select and operate equipment suitable for hunting rabbits in the darkness.

Practical Skills:

The practical skills that you will learn from this chapter are the ability to set up a night vision scope on your rifle and zero it to a range of 25yd. You will also be able to set up a high-powered mini hunting light.

Time Period Required For Mastery Of Practical Skills:

Four to six hours.

GEN 1 NIGHT VISION SCOPES

In this chapter I am going to outline how to set up and use a Gen 1 night vision scope. However, many shooters will say that I am out of date and that all the really good new night vision scopes coming onto the market today are of the digital type. I am not about to argue that a Gen 1 scope is going to outdo one of the state-of-the-art digital night vision scopes, but digital night scopes are very expensive pieces of equipment, costing around £1000 at least and, in my opinion, this is too much money for my night hunting activities.

I do not hunt for sport, but to harvest meat from the wild animals that I can take for free. Whilst I accept that I have to spend a lot of money for a rifle, I do not accept that I have to spend £1000 for a scope to enable me to take rabbits in the dark, there being far more cost-effective options available. For me, the objective of taking meat from the wild is to radically reduce household bills, as I live an independent lifestyle producing and harvesting all that I possibly can for myself.

An average household spends about £100 per week on food, which equates to £5200 per year, without even taking into account special occasions, which takes the cost even higher. Of that, about one quarter will account for meat, which is £1300 and so, by taking all my meat from the wild, I can reduce my yearly expenditure by over £1000.

You can see that the economics of hunting are of great importance to my philosophy on life, so you will understand why I look at the cost of all my equipment and figure out how long it will take me to see a return on the cost of my purchases. I hunt rabbits for only six months of the year – from October through to March – the reason for this being that winter rabbits provide the best eating and the best pelts. Summer pelts are no use whatsoever and, if the rabbits are left to breed freely during the summer months they produce a healthy crop that can be harvested over the winter.

My night hunting activities then cover a period of twenty-eight weeks, which means that if I have two hunts per week, and take on average five rabbits per hunt, I will shoot 280 rabbits during the night hunting session. Some years ago I used to have lots of contact with game dealers and, back then, a rabbit was worth £1. The price has gone up somewhat since then and must now be around £2 and so, in monetary terms, I take about £560 worth of rabbits per year. I like all my equipment to have paid for itself in the first year but, if I were to spend £1000 buying a digital night vision scope, it would take two years at least before it had paid for itself.

I say two years but, in fact, it would be more like three because the scope cannot work by itself; for true, undetected night hunting you also need a night vision monocular or binocular in order to scout the ground to find your quarry. You may say but I can scout the ground by looking through my scope, but that is an absolute contravention of good rifle practice. The golden rule is never point your barrel at something that you are not willing to destroy. However, you cannot know if you are willing to destroy something until you have identified it, which requires a night vision device working independently of the rifle.

Scanning a field for rabbits with a loaded rifle could have you covering anything from the farmer's cat to another human being; both examples are totally unacceptable. Even if I unload my rifle and am, therefore, no longer pointing a loaded weapon, this is still not acceptable. Even with unloaded weapons, accidents occur due to pellets or rounds accidentally being left in the breech. The other problem with using the rifle to scout the ground for quarry is that rifles are not made to be binoculars; they are made to deliver ammunition and are too cumbersome for the task of scouting. Good night vision binoculars will cost just over £500, and a really good night vision monocular about £230.

The NEXGEN 4X, sold by Deben, is the perfect example of a night vision monocular that will enable you to scout the ground up to 150m ahead, allowing you to clearly plan your stalk. 4× magnification on a monocular is the ideal level of magnification for scouting purposes and is the level of magnification that American special forces used to have on their Litton M975 night vision

binoculars. These binoculars could clearly identify the features of a man at just over 1000m on a moonlit night.

If you do not have a night vision monocular or binocular, then you will need to use a light to scout for rabbits, which rather nullifies having a night vision scope. The cost of the night scope must therefore be added to the cost of a night vision monocular or binocular, taking the cost of the total digital night vision package up to between £1300 and £1500. A Gen 1 scope can be purchased from Deben for £469, and a monocular for £229, bringing the whole package in for £698 – half the price you would have to pay for a complete night vision rig with a digital scope.

I think I have established why I prefer to use what some may consider the old style Gen 1 night vision riflescope. The Gen 1 is not as sophisticated as the digital night vision scopes, nor does it offer the clarity of image produced by a digital scope, but a Gen 1 scope works and is a very effective bag filler; the rabbits being taken cleanly without any light disturbance to the environment. I really like using night vision equipment because it allows you to move about in the darkness like natural predators, such as the fox and the owl, and to use the darkness as a weapon from which you can strike unseen and unobserved.

The 350 Guardian Gen 1 Night Vision Scope

Deben, the company that produce the excellent Hawke range of scopes, also provide a small, very select range of night vision scopes, among which is the 350 Guardian Gen 1 night vision scope.

I have used this scope and found it to be a very effective tool. Although it only offers 2.5× magnification, this is sufficient at the 25 to 30yd range, which is my optimum range for night hunting. I find it easy to stalk down to such a range when using night vision equipment, as there is no light to give away my location.

A lot of airgun shooters will dismiss 2.5×

magnification, claiming that they could not put together a sufficiently tight grouping with such a small amount of magnification. If that is the case then that shooter is not ready for advanced hunting; you should be able to achieve at least a 1in grouping, or less, with 2.5× magnification out to ranges of 30yd consistently, without too much effort.

During the nineties, Navy SEALs used a night vision scope, which they zeroed to 100m. The magnification on the Litton scope they used was a rather unusual 1.55× magnification and, although the target of the SEAL is obviously much larger than a rabbit, they could effectively engage targets with the precision delivery of rounds out to just below 200yd, with just the small amount of magnification that the scope offered.

Tight groupings, and the precision placement of pellets out to 30yd, are extremely achievable for the competent marksman with 2.5× magnification and the fine cross hairs used on the Guardian's reticle. The reticle in the Guardian is of the 30/30 duplex type, with very fine centre cross hairs that are illuminated in red, allowing for a strong contrast against the rabbit, which appears in the ocular lens as a green image.

The red cross hairs present such a vivid contrast because the rabbit is effectively turned green by the scope. This allows for a very precise placement of the aim point on the kill zone of the rabbit, despite the low magnification, ensuring for consistent first shot kills. The cross hairs provide a much more defined contrast than you get when lamping, even if your scope is equipped with an illuminated reticle, because the red illumination does not contrast as well with the natural brown colour of a rabbit as it does with the green colour of a rabbit in a night vision scope.

The Guardian weighs in at 1.27kg, which a lot of airgun shooters would baulk at, arguing that the scope is far too heavy, and it is true that the new digital night vision scopes are lighter. However, to put this into perspective, the Guardian is 1270g and the day scope that I recommend, the Sidewinder, with a 30mm tube, is 780g: so the Guardian is only 490g heavier than the day scope. This is hardly a huge amount of additional weight and, besides which, if optimum accuracy is to be achieved, every single shot should be taken from a supported firing position. For me this means the prone position when night hunting, with the aid of a front-mounted bipod, so the weight of the scope is an irrelevance as the rifle is self-supporting when fired from such a position.

The Guardian fits to a Weaver rail and therefore, if you have set your rifle up as explained in Chapter Two, using a Weaver rail you can swap from day scope to night scope with the greatest of ease in as little as two minutes. Simply place the scope into a position on the rail that has been marked as the scope's zero location, and with just a couple of shots having to be fired to check the zero to ensure that the scope has not been disturbed. This, however, is just a precautionary measure, as the Guardian is such a robust little scope that it never seems to lose zero, even if it does happen to get knocked about a bit.

The ability to move from night vision to day scope with such ease, because both scopes are utilizing the Weaver system, is a real plus point and means that the rifle can be used during the day for pest control work against feral pigeons, and then quickly set up to take a few rabbits when night falls. The effective targeting range of the 350 Guardian night vision scope is 100m, which is in excess of the ranges that you will be hunting with using an air rifle.

One point worth noting is that a clearer image will be received if you hunt by moonlight, rather than hunting under cloudy conditions, so it is best to coordinate your night hunting expeditions with the appearance of a full moon. The reason for this is that the night vision scope requires a light source to see in the dark, and the greater the light source, the greater the clarity of the image. The light source utilized by the scope is the infrared illuminator mounted on top of the scope, which works just like a torch only it sends out a beam of light on the infrared scale, which is invisible to the eye.

lens cap/
daylight filter

infrared
illuminator

elevation
turret

diopter
adjustment
ring

windage
turret

focusing
ring

power
button

reticule brightness
adjuster

battery
housing

*The 350 Guardian
night vision scope.*

adjustable fixation rail

*The adjustable
fixation rail.*

The focusing ring.

focusing ring

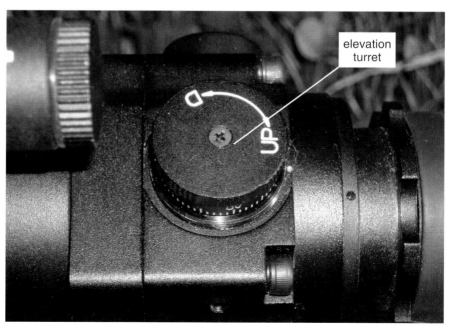

elevation turret

UP

The elevation turret.

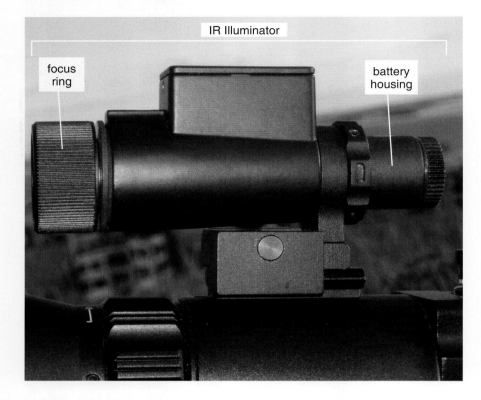

The IR illuminator.

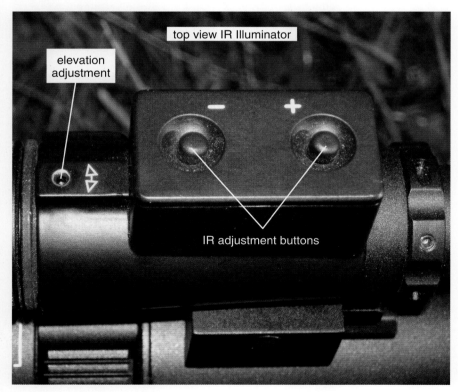

A top view of the IR illuminator.

*The reticle
brightness adjuster.*

reticle brightness adjuster

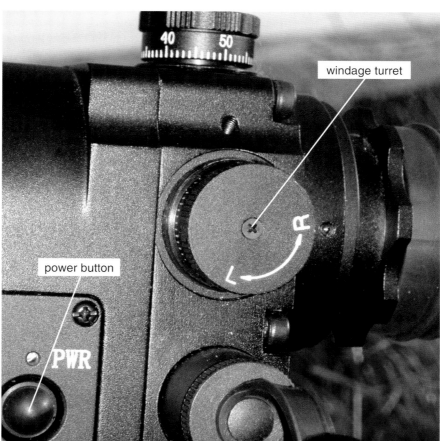

windage turret

power button

*The windage turret
and power button.*

The appearance of an image as seen through a night vision scope.

As to range finding with a night vision scope, there are two indicators that are of value: firstly the scope should be focused to engage targets at 30yd (I will cover the procedure involved in focusing the scope shortly), and any target above or below this distance will appear out of focus. The second indicator is the cross hairs, which, although not possessing mil dots, can be used to bracket the rabbit in the traditional manner.

Now we come to setting up the 350 Guardian on your rifle, which is fairly straightforward. Firstly mount it onto the Weaver rail, and then take the rifle off to the range, with a target set up at 30yd and the rifle supported on a front-mounted bipod. Begin by focusing the scope, which involves turning the diopter ring clockwise until it stops. Then, look through the scope, which involves having the eye in contact with the rubber eyepiece. The contact with the eyepiece should be full but gentle, a point that you need to bear in mind when locating the scope on the Weaver rail. Make sure that you do not place it too far forward, as this will crane the neck unnaturally forward in order to contact the eyepiece, producing muscular tension that will undermine your attempts to produce accurate shots.

Looking through the scope at the target you have placed at 30yd, which needs to be a bold and clearly identifiable image, turn the diopter ring counter-clockwise until the grain that you see in the ocular lens becomes

sharp. The grain is a bit like the fuzz you used to get on old TV screens when you tuned them in by turning a knob. The aim is to get the grain as sharp as possible, which occurs when they become uniform and tightly bunched. Do not worry if the image does not become too sharp, it is the quality of the grain that you are adjusting with the diopter; the sharpness of the image comes about by rotating the focus ring till the image assumes clarity.

Once the focusing is done it is set for a range of 30yd. If you require the scope to operate at longer or lesser ranges, then you will need to move the focus ring to set it up for that particular range, but the diopter ring, once focused, does not need to be moved again. The focusing is done in daylight with the rubber lens cap – which also serves as a daylight filter – in place. The lens cap allows sufficient light to enter the scope for it to see in daylight but also ensures that not too much light enters which would cause it to shut down. The scope has an inbuilt safety device to prevent it becoming damaged by the entry of bright light, which it cannot cope with. Needless to say, in order to be focused the scope has to be switched on.

The scope focused during daylight may well need a very slight adjustment to the focus ring in night-time conditions, just to bring the image to optimum clarity due to the difference between daytime and night-time conditions. However, do not make any adjustment to the diopter ring, once that is focused leave it alone, unless the focus of the grain loses its sharpness.

Once the scope is focused it is time to zero the cross hair in to 30yd. Again, this operation is carried out during daylight, with the daylight filter in place. A lot of shooters think they have to wait until night-time to zero in a night vision scope, but that is a popular misconception. Zeroing is carried out as normal, with the turrets being located under substantial, military-type, screw-off dust caps. And do not forget to centralize the turrets before beginning the zeroing process.

The scope is powered by a single, three volt battery – a CR123 or equivalent – which gives between ten and twenty hours of operation. Always carry a spare battery in your pocket so that if you have misjudged the amount of work the battery has done, or it turns out to be faulty, the hunt does not have to be abandoned. The IR illuminator, which is also powered by a CR123 battery, simply clamps to the Picantinny rail on top of the scope and is switched on every time you use the scope. It should be obvious, but is surprising how many shooters forget to remove the lens cap before taking the shot; leave it in place, however, whilst making the stalk as any scratching to the lens will inhibit clarity; protect the lens and it will never let you down.

Mini Hunting Lamps And Scopes To Use With Them

It has to be said that the use of night vision equipment is the most enjoyable way to move around in the darkness, but plenty of shooters simply cannot justify the cost of night vision equipment, even the more affordable Gen 1 type scope, but such hunters can still engage in night hunting by using one of the mini hunting lamps on the market, in conjunction with a suitable scope. When it comes to a lamp there are literally hundreds to choose from and some of them are very expensive, costing several hundred pounds for the lamp alone.

The TK12 mounted with the front of the torch level with the objective lens.

However, I have come across a phenomenal little lamp that costs just £116 for the lamp, batteries, battery charger, rubber scope mount and red filter. The lamp I refer to is the Fenix TK12, a small lamp that fits into the palm of your hand, but fires out a tight beam of light, like a burst of sunlight, that illuminates the ground for 100m in front of the shooter. A single, 2400mAh battery giving out 3.7v, the battery offering a clear two hours of bright light, powers the lamp.

The beauty of such small batteries is that you can carry three or four of them in your pocket to provide you with a spare six to eight hours of light, and the batteries are so light that you hardly notice they are in your pocket. The batteries provided with the torch are rechargeable, taking just two hours to fully charge and, in my experience, they just keep charging all through the hunting season, never losing the slightest bit of power. The TK12 is tough, weather-proof and, most of all, dependable; there is nothing worse than being in the middle of a night hunting expedition and the lamp you are using suddenly goes out on you.

Many hunters still use the large lamps with a 250 to 500m beam, powered by batteries the size of a car battery, and which are a pain to carry about on a hunt. Such lamps were never necessary as the air rifle has a maximum range in the hands of an advanced airgun marksman of 40 to 45yd, so a beam of 250 to 500m is totally superfluous. Such lamps were made for use with firearms and are not necessary for the airgun hunter. A small lamp with a short, narrow beam is much more in keeping with the needs of the airgun hunter and, with a small lamp like the Fenix TK12, you drastically reduce the amount of light pollution and disturbance you produce, which should be another factor that you take into account.

Just the other day a farmer was lamping for foxes about two to three miles from my smallholding. I could see the beam of his light cutting across the land and falling just short of my field. The lamp scanned for its quarry like an anti-aircraft lamp, causing disturbance to the wildlife, livestock and houses that the beam fell across.

Causing this kind of light disturbance can make you very unpopular, which is why I now exclusively use the smaller TK12, with its much less intrusive beam. I further diminish the disturbance factor by fitting a red or green filter to the front of the lamp. If you look at the difference between the headlights of a car and the red brake lights, you will see that red light offers a much softer beam.

Using the TK12, with a red filter mounted on a Nite Eye scope, I can take 40yd long-range shots in the prone position, with the rifle supported with a front-mounted bipod. The reason I do this with the lamp, and not with the night vision scope, is simply that the TK12 with the Nite Eye scope provides an image of greater clarity than the Gen 1 night vision scope. The aiming grid on the Nite Eye, which can be the 10× ½ mil dot, the Map 6A, or the SR6, is a much more sophisticated aiming device than the aiming grid on the Gen 1 night vision scope. This means that a much more precise placement of the aim point on the kill zone can be made, allowing for a very high degree of precision with the shot placement, which means that the range can be increased to 40yd with confidence.

For the best results, the TK12 should be mounted as far forward on the scope as possible, preferably with the front of the torch level with the objective lens. To prevent the beam from the torch causing whiteout in the scope, fit the sunshade to the scope. In my experience the best magnification setting for night-time hunting is 9×, and the preferred zero when using a lamp is 30yd. To attach the lamp to the scope you should use a rubber clamp. I have recently discovered this brilliantly simple little device, which has a rubber cup that goes onto the scope and another cup that goes around the lamp, the whole thing being held together with Velcro.

The clamp can literally be set up in seconds, with no need to tighten any fiddly little screws, making it easy to get ready for

The rubber scope clamp.

a night hunting expedition. As with many of the best ideas, the rubber scope mount is an extremely simple idea but, after having used it, I shall never again bother with the fiddly metal scope mounts, which are a chore to attach to the scope.

If you want to increase the level of illumination, you can set up a second torch on the rear part of the scope tube, giving you a car headlight effect. You can also use the TK12 in conjunction with a Gen 1 night vision scope if you wish to use the night vision scope on a dark, moonless night, when the image offered by the scope will have less clarity, due to the lack of natural night light. Simply attach the TK12 to the barrel of your gun using the scope clamp, which fits neatly

around the silencer, and fit it with a red or green filter and you have a very effective light source that will greatly enhance the clarity of the night vision scope.

Under no circumstances should you use a rifle with a scope-mounted lamp to scout the ground for rabbits, for exactly the same reason that you do not use a rifle-mounted night vision scope to scout for rabbits: because it is a very dangerous bit of poor rifle practice. To scout the ground you should be carrying a second lamp and, for this purpose, you could not do better than using the EB21, a very light lamp, weighing just 90g, but with the capacity to search the ground for up to 100m ahead of the shooter and costing just over £30.

The rubber scope clamp fitted to the silencer.

Chapter 5
Fitness Training for the Shooter and Some Notes on Camouflage

CHAPTER OBJECTIVES

Knowledge:

In this chapter you will gain an understanding of the relationship between shooting performance and fitness, and learn about the way your quarry views its world in relation to appropriate levels of camouflage.

Practical Skills:

As a result of studying this chapter you will be able to perform exercises designed to improve the hunting shooter's performance. And you will be able to camouflage yourself in such a way that you can evade detection by your quarry.

FITNESS PROGRAMME

Every competitive field of shooting, from trap shooting, to target pistol shooting, recognizes that increased fitness can improve performance. Even sports that were traditionally considered somewhat sedentary, such as snooker, also now see that fitness is a key factor to the achieving of advanced levels of sporting performance. Fitness as regards shooting will improve coordination, breath control, muscle control and concentration and will make the shooter more able to deal with fatigue and stress.

The ability to overcome fatigue is vital to the hunter's performance in the field, as most hunts involve walking long distances. I will easily cover four to five miles on a hunt, usually in poor weather, when wet or

cold conditions are at work trying to break my morale and endurance. The RAF survival training school, responsible for training pilots to survive in a hostile environment if they are shot down behind enemy lines, states that the quickest and most complete breaker of the pilot's morale is the rain; one of the most effective weapons to combat its effects is the toughness that is brought about by physical training.

The ability to overcome fatigue is paramount in terms of accuracy on the shoot. It is easy at the beginning of a shoot to place a pellet very precisely in the brain of the target rabbit but, as the miles add up, going up and down hills, across ditches and over fences, with the wind cutting into you, the accuracy can very rapidly disappear if you do not have the physical condition required to overcome the physical stresses of the hunt.

Tired muscles, when required to provide support to the rifle, quiver like jelly, making the placement of the cross hairs very challenging. With tiredness also comes a lessening of concentration and a decrease in coordination. This is why shots that the unfit shooter might have achieved with relative ease at the beginning of a shoot are missed with regularity as the shoot progresses, and why the wounding of the target quarry begins to occur.

Those who wish to engage live targets at the limits of the rifle and shooter's abilities at 40yd must have a level of fitness that enables them to perform at the same high level of marksmanship from the beginning, right through to the end of the shoot, no matter how many hills or miles they have covered. The fitness programme that follows has, therefore, been specifically tailored to meet the needs of the airgun hunter.

Fitness for hunting needs to be divided into two categories: fitness for the act of shooting, and fitness for the physical exertions involved in covering large areas of country in search of quarry.

For shooting we need to address conditioning of the eye, improving muscle control in the upper body, improving breath control, improving coordination and developing flexibility so that shooting positions can be taken easily without tension appearing in the body.

For covering large areas of ground we need to address the development of the muscles in the leg, and the improvement of the cardiovascular system. There is also a need to develop back strength because the hunter can end up carrying considerable weights over several miles. An adult rabbit weighs approximately 1.2kg, but big bucks can weigh as much as 2kg. Therefore, a bag of ten rabbits – which is quiet achievable on good hunting grounds – will place a weight of between 12 and 15kg on the hunter's back. Add on the weight of the rifle at about 4kg and you have a combined weight of 20kg, which is a considerable load if you have to carry it for several miles back to your vehicle. So you need to have the prerequisite strength for this task or you'll end up giving yourself a mild heart attack bringing home your bag.

Shooting Fitness

The following set of exercises is designed to improve the performance of the shooter in relation to the use of a rifle. The programme is divided into four areas as follows:

- Flexibility
- Upper body strength
- Coordination
- Cardiovascular fitness relating to breath control

I shall give a brief explanation of all the exercises that make up the fitness programme, so that you can be clear how they are performed. I shall then detail the fitness regimes, showing how many are required of each exercise, and how often they should be performed. Some of the exercises involve the use of light weights, and for these you need to purchase a small 20kg set of weights that has both dumbbells and a barbell, which will cost no more than £30 to £40.

The Hand

The following exercises will develop strength and flexibility in the hand, so as to improve trigger control. These exercises will also help to minimize the stiffening effects of old age, in order to prolong your shooting career.

Simple Finger Stretch

Stretch the thumb over to the base of the little finger, then stretch each finger one after the other, as far as you can toward the wrist.

The Rubber Ball Squeeze

Use a soft rubber ball, such as a squash ball, and place it in the palm of the hand, then squeeze it firmly.

Fingertip Suspension

Find a suitable beam, doorframe or other overhanging structure that can support your body weight. Take a fingertip grip on the beam, and then raise your knees up so as to suspend your body from the fingertips. Hold, building up to a count of thirty.

Some shooters may find this exercise too demanding to start with; if that is the case, wait until your fingers are strong enough to carry out this exercise.

Finger Curls

In a sitting position, place the back of your wrists against your knees holding a barbell, now open and close the fingers. Start this exercise with no weight on the barbell then, when you feel you have sufficient strength in the fingers, you can add weight to the bar, starting with a 1kg disc on either end of the bar and working up to a 5kg disc on either end.

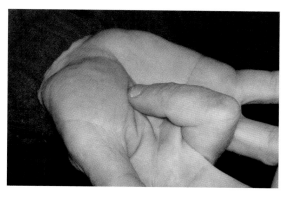

Simple finger stretches (ABOVE)

Rubber ball squeeze (ABOVE)

Fingertip suspension (LEFT)

Side bends (LEFT)

Finger curls (ABOVE)

Trunk rotation (LEFT)

Dorsal raises (ABOVE)

Side lunges
(LEFT)

Front lunges (ABOVE)

Toe touch
(LEFT)

Shoulder press (ABOVE)

*Side bends with
dumbbells* (RIGHT)

Chest press (ABOVE)

Barbell curls (ABOVE)

Dead lift (ABOVE)

Sit ups (ABOVE)

Drop squat (ABOVE)

Abdominal twists (ABOVE)

Flexibility in the Trunk, Back and Legs

Do not rush any of these exercises; the idea is to stretch as far as you can comfortably go. Do not try and go beyond your body's capabilities, or you will end up damaging yourself, rather than improving your flexibility. You should never stretch cold muscles, which is why every stretching session should be preceded by a short, one-mile, jog or brisk walk.

Side Bends

Stand with feet shoulder width apart, and then bend to the right, lowering the right arm towards the knee. Then move it outwards, at the same time move the left arm up to the waist.

Trunk Rotation

With your feet shoulder width apart, place your hands on your hips then rotate the trunk as far as you can to the right.

Dorsal Raises

Lie flat on the ground, or on a bench, with your stomach to the floor and your arms behind your back. Then, gently use the muscles of the back to raise the head and upper body fractionally off the ground. Hold for one second, and then lower your head and upper body gently back to the floor.

Side Lunges

Stand with your legs about shoulder width apart, then bend the right knee, taking the body as far as possible to the right, then return to the centre and do the same to the left.

Front Lunges

Stand with your feet roughly shoulder width apart, then lift the right foot and place it about 3ft in front of the left foot and bend the right leg at the knee, as far as is comfortably possible.

Toe Touch

Stand with your feet together. Then, when you are comfortable, reach down with both hands and try to get as close to your feet as you can without straining.

Building Strength in the Upper Body, the Legs and the Back

Weightlifting builds strength in both muscles and bones, and is one of the best forms of exercise for combating the degenerative effects of aging. However, common sense must be used when lifting weights or you will do yourself serious damage; the key rule being do not lift more than you can handle. These are weight training exercises not weightlifting exercises: weight training being used to condition muscles, whereas weightlifting is the sport of lifting extremely heavy weights. The purpose of the following exercises is not to lift as much as you possibly can, but to lift sufficient to condition the muscles to the required degree.

Seated Shoulder Press

To perform this exercise you will need a weight training bench. Load up a barbell with a weight that you can handle. You want no more than a 10kg disc on either end of the bar, but if this is too heavy for you then start with 2kg or 5kg discs. Sit on the end of your bench with a wide grip on the dumbbell, which should be placed under the chin. Then, keeping the back straight, push the bar up until the arms lock out, and then lower it back down to the starting position.

Chest Press

For this exercise you will need a weight training bench. Place a barbell in the cups of the bench, loaded up with a weight that you can comfortably manage. This should not be more than 15kg on either end of the bar, but if that is beyond you, then start with 5kg or 10kg on either end. Lie on the bench and take hold of the weight bar with a wide grip, then lift the bar out of the cups and lower it down to the chest, holding in on the chest for about a second, then raise it back up.

Side Bends With Dumbbells

Load up a dumbbell with a 2.5kg disc on either end. Then, standing with feet shoulder width apart and a dumbbell in the right

The muscles that are worked by specific weight training exercises.

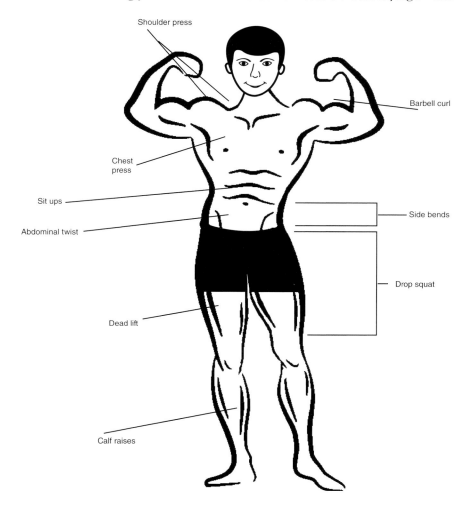

hand, bend to the right as far as you can, raising the left arm up as you bend.

Barbell Curls

Place no more than a 10kg disc on either end of the barbell; if this is too heavy for you then start out with a 2.5kg or 5kg disc. Hold the bar shoulder width apart and curl it up towards the chest. The key to producing results is not to rush the movement but to take it slowly both in the raising and lowering of the bar.

Dead Lift

Be very careful carrying out this exercise because, if you place more weight on the bar than you are able to handle, you can damage the back muscles, which could put you out of action for months. Start with a 5kg disc on either end of a barbell. If even this is too heavy for you, then start with a 2.5kg disc. When you have developed sufficient strength you can move up to a 10kg disc, or even a 20kg disc. Stand with your feet shoulder width apart, with the bar on the ground in front of you. Bend from the waist and slightly bend the knees, allowing you to reach down and take hold of the bar with your hands, shoulder width apart, with one palm facing inward and the other outward. At all times keep the back straight. Raise yourself back up until the bar is in front of your thighs. Do not lock the knees.

EXERCISE	TIMES PER WEEK	REPETITIONS [Each time you work out]	TOTAL REPETITIONS PER WEEK
Simple finger stretch	5	5 each hand	25 each hand
Rubber ball squeeze	5	5 each hand	25 each hand
Fingertip suspension	5	3	15
Finger curls	5	3 sets of 10	150

Time period required for the completion of one exercise routine five minutes.

EXERCISE	TIMES PER WEEK	REPETITIONS [Each time you workout]	TOTAL REPETITIONS PER WEEK
Side bends	5	10 either side	50 either side
Trunk rotations	5	10 each way	50 each way
Dorsal raises	5	3 sets of 10	150
Side lunges	5	10 either side	50 either side
Front lunges	5	10 each leg	50 each leg
Toe touch	5	5	50

Time period required for the completion of one exercise routine ten minutes.

EXERCISES	TIMES PER WEEK	REPETITIONS [Each time you workout]	TOTAL REPETITIONS PER WEEK
Shoulder press	1	3×10	30
Chest press	1	3×10	30
Side bends with dumbbell	1	3×10 each side	30 each side
Barbell curls	1	3×10	30
Dead lift	1	3×10	30
Drop squat	1	3×10	30
Calf raises	1	3×20	60
Sit ups	1	50	100
Abdominal twist	1	50	100

Time period required for the completion of the exercise routine forty-five minutes.

Drop Squat

Place a 10kg disc on either end of a barbell; if this is too much for you then begin with a 5kg disc. Lift the bar and place it behind your neck, resting on your shoulders with the grip nice and wide. Keeping the entire torso straight, slowly bend the knees, taking the body into a shallow squat, which you want to hold for about a second, then raise gently back to the starting position.

Calf Raises

Stand with your feet together, and then place your hands on a wall for support. Now rise slowly up onto your tiptoes, and then come back down onto your heels.

Sit Ups

Lie on your back with your knees raised and your hands behind your head, then raise the head and shoulders up off the ground nice and slowly, then lower back to the starting position.

Abdominal Twist

Lie as before, with your knees raised and your hands behind your head, only this time when you raise up the shoulders and head, twist the right elbow toward the left knee and then, next time, twist the left elbow to the right knee.

Exercises for Cardiovascular Fitness

An improvement in cardiovascular fitness will increase your stamina, allowing you to cover large amounts of ground without becoming fatigued. Cardiovascular fitness will also help you to improve breath control, enabling you take a longer and more relaxed hold. Brisk walking can develop cardiovascular fitness, especially if this is done over hilly ground. Since nearly every airgun hunter I know owns a dog, the opportunity is there to turn a dog walk into a serious bit of training. Instead of ambling along behind the dog, stride out, moving crisply across the ground and making your body sweat. A one-hour dog walk should see you covering approximately two miles and, if you do this five or six times a week, you will radically improve cardiovascular fitness.

Once you have acquired a level of walking fitness, place a rucksack on your back twice a week that contains a weight of 5kg, in time increasing that weight to 10kg. This will build up your carrying endurance, allowing you to carry your bag of rabbits easily from the field. For those wishing a greater degree of cardiovascular fitness, you will need to up the pace and go from walking to jogging, taking a two-mile jog, three times a week. Not only will improved cardiovascular performance enhance your hunting abilities, it will also increase your lifespan so it is something well worth doing.

Exercises for Coordination

The following selection of exercises will improve your coordination: skipping, working with a speed ball and any kind of racket game, such as squash or badminton. Any one of these activities, practised a couple of times a week, will improve your coordination.

Understand How Camouflage Works In Relation to Target Quarry

Most shooters address the question of camouflage from a human's perspective, aiming for total concealment, believing that this is necessary to overcome the quarry's naturally alert instincts and senses, but this is not the case. For example, if a rabbit or bird sees a rifle barrel or scope sticking up through the grass, it does not think to itself: 'That is a rifle and I must take cover or I will be shot'; the rifle is an unfamiliar object but, as long as it does not move, the rabbit will soon get used to it.

However, many shooters think that the rifle must be made invisible, covering it in burlap, or having it painted in camouflage. This is certainly necessary if you are a sniper and your target is another human being, able to carry out deductive reasoning, but we are hunters and not snipers and so we do not need to camouflage our equipment, or ourselves, to the same degree.

In the following photograph I am wearing a ghillie suit to disguise the human form, but I have not bothered to place any camouflage on my hands. Some shooters would say that I am giving away my position but, again, they are looking at the camouflage from a human perspective, not an animal one. The rabbit does not see my hand and deduce that I am attached to it. In the same way, a man mounted on a horse can ride right into the middle of a herd of wild deer and they do not take any notice of him, seemingly seeing him as part of the horse, rather than deducing that he is a human being mounted on a horse. So there is no need for anti-glare finishes on your rifle and scope and no need for camouflage that makes you totally invisible.

I did some experiments hunting feral pigeons, which are just about the most alert quarry that you can go in pursuit of. I wore ordinary, outdoor clothing, with my face completely bare and, when the pigeons saw me within 50yd of their position they took flight. However, when I covered my face with a ghillie hood, I was able to get across open ground and take up a shooting position within 30yd of the target birds, suggesting to me that it is the face that is the identifying feature that birds respond to; once it is covered, this removes their suspicion. It is not the rifle or the human body that places them on the alert, but the human face; hide it and you remove the trigger to the quarry's flight mechanism.

So camouflage is not about hiding every single part of your anatomy from view; there is no need to wear camouflage boots,

An exposed hand does not give away your position to the quarry.

trousers and jacket, instead concentrate on the face and then the torso, using a ghillie jacket to distort the human form.

Understanding how to move correctly is of more value than all the camouflage in the world, and it costs an awful lot less. To understand how to move, you have to know how the quarry sees and senses its world. The following comments are going to relate essentially to the rabbit, as this is the main prize for the long-range hunter; if you wish to learn more about the hunting of birds then refer to my previous book about airgun shooting for pest control.

The rabbit has a wonderful sight capacity for movement, but is relatively poor at seeing stationary objects, and is unable to focus on them for more than a few moments. Therefore, the key to getting close to rabbits is to avoid fast movements; when the rabbit looks in your direction, freeze just like a fox. A fox stalking a rabbit will often freeze mid-stride, with a paw raised in the air when the rabbit looks in its direction, not placing the paw to the ground until the rabbit looks in another direction.

Dropping to the floor or rushing to cover may look very dramatic, but it is the worst thing that you can do; you are far better off in the open, standing as still as a statue, than making a dash for cover. When the rabbit is not watching, you get as low to the ground as you possibly can, preferably the prone position, and move very slowly into the required range. The rabbit does have a magnificent sense of smell but, in my experience, it does not flee when it picks up human scent, it simply becomes very alert.

The rabbit's first response to perceived danger is to crouch down as low as it possibly can to the ground, with its ears pressed firmly against its back, making it extremely camouflaged. It does this in order to conceal its location, as it knows when it runs its position is betrayed and the predator will commence pursuit. So, when a rabbit's nostrils pick up human scent, if it feels in any danger it will first try to hide and, only if

you give it further cause for concern by making a rapid movement, will it take to its legs and run.

Letting the rabbit receive your scent is therefore not a problem. Rabbits also possess an exceptional sense of hearing and, whilst they respond to sound in the same way as they do to scent, you do not want to sound like an army of elephants, snapping every twig you come across underfoot, so tread softly and slowly, which will also aid balance and prevent you from making sudden movements.

The best way to move is to use the Indian glide, which involves placing the heel on the ground first, rather than the toe, and keeping the foot nice and close to the ground. It is amazing how many shooters actually end up missing a rabbit close to them because they do not know how to search the ground in front of them. This involves searching the ground ahead using a very good pair of binoculars, before you move on to it to identify the target quarry. This is termed 'scouting', meaning to observe and gather information without being detected. When on the ground you have previously scouted, you need to use rays of vision, rather than bands of vision, to make the search for quarry. Bands of vision are what most people naturally use to search an area; this involves beginning the search at close range, then scanning from side to side, gradually increasing the distance.

Vision rays involve moving the focus from near to far, then shifting it laterally, then moving it from far to near, and then repeating the process a number of times across a specified arc that covers the area of ground you wish to search.

Success in the stalk therefore involves light camouflage that conceals the face and breaks up the upper body shape, combined with skilful, precise and deliberately slow movements. This is something that needs to be practised – slow movement is not something that comes naturally to modern man, always in a rush to get everywhere more and more quickly.

Visual bands.

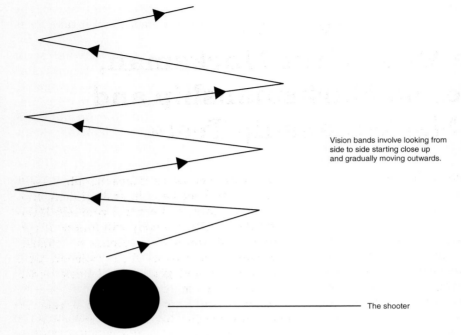

Vision bands involve looking from
side to side starting close up
and gradually moving outwards.

The shooter

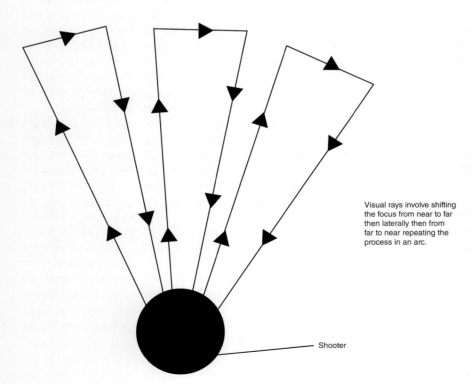

Visual rays involve shifting
the focus from near to far
then laterally then from
far to near repeating the
process in an arc.

Shooter

Visual rays.

Chapter 6
The Mind of the Marksman,
Notes on Marksmanship and
Marksmanship Tests

CHAPTER OBJECTIVES

Knowledge:

This chapter will outline the mindset that the advanced airgun hunter needs to have, in order to achieve the accurate placement of long-range shots. You will also learn some key facts about the techniques of marksmanship.

Practical:

Through extensive periods spent on the range, you will develop the skill required to place groupings of 12mm at 40yd consistently.

Range Time Required 100hrs (four hours per week over six months)

THE MINDSET OF THE MARKSMAN

In order to shoot like a skilled marksman, you must be able to think like one and, in order to think at all, you must first suppress any excitement you might feel. Many shooters become very excited when they spot their quarry; as a result their pulse goes up, they begin to sweat more heavily, their muscles begin to quiver and their concentration becomes erratic; consequently the shot is missed.

It does not matter how well set up the rifle is, or how well zeroed the scope is, if the shooter's heart is beating like a drum and their muscles are quivering like jelly. Excitement, though natural, is completely

counterproductive and it must be suppressed; you have to become cold and clinical, like the fox or hawk, and control yourself: if the mind stays calm, the body will follow. If you should find yourself overcome by sudden excitement, then pause for a moment, take deep breaths and get yourself back under control before you proceed.

A successful shot starts with a relaxed body, any tension brought about by excitement or doubt will ruin the shot long before the trigger is even touched. Doubt, and by that I mean doubting your ability to make the shot, is going to subconsciously trigger hesitation and tension, both of which will ruin the shot. The only way to remove doubts from the shooter's mind is to spend hours on the range, until consistent groupings at extreme range are achieved. Go far beyond what is legitimate in the field and engage paper targets at ranges of 50 and 55yd. When you can put together a 15mm grouping on a target at such an extreme range, then your confidence will go through the roof and all doubt will be banished, removing the subconscious hesitation that can have such a marked effect on accuracy.

When taking a shot it is important to visualize the shot: see the shot in your mind's eye leaving the rifle, before you pull the trigger, imagine its trajectory and envisage its strike point on the quarry. This exercise only takes a fraction of a second, yet it somehow reaches past the mind of the shooter and engages a deeper level of concentration, coming from the soul.

Martial artists have utilized the visualization technique, in their use of weapons like the bow and spear, for thousands of years and it has taken their accuracy from good to superlative.

It is imperative to become part of the rifle, sensing its rhythm and reading what the projectile will do, and visualization is key to achieving this objective. Another important facet of the marksman's mindset is awareness. The shooter who, when looking through the scope, is constantly taken by surprise by the movement of the rabbit, will never be able to deliver a precisely placed shot to the kill zone. Reading the rabbit's behaviour and knowing what it is going to do, before it does it, is key to the timing of the shot.

On a paper target there is no issue with timing, as the target will stay where you put it. However, a rabbit is a very active creature and can move just as you release the shot, causing a miss that can be lived with or worse, an injury, which is not so easy to live with. Timing the shot to perfection is, therefore, imperative, which means having the ability to read the rabbit's movements, so that you can tell when it is going to be still.

By knowing when this will come about, you can take up the first stage of trigger engagement, fractionally before the point at which you anticipate the rabbit will become still, taking a hesitation in the trigger pull so that you can finalize the aim. Then, when you are fully satisfied and confident that the intended shot will kill, you make the final pull on the trigger, which will release the sear and send the shot on its way.

You do not have to take up the first and second stages of the trigger engagement in one long pull. The technique of pausing between the first and second stage of the pull is a well-established technique that is taught to all military snipers. The technique is referred to as the 'interrupted pull', and it is designed to meet the challenges presented by a target likely to move during the process of aligning the shot. Though there is a pause, it is only a momentary one and is not intended to be utilized for minutes at a time.

To control a trigger like this requires a high degree of feeling from the shooter; you have to know, from the feel of the trigger alone, when you have reached the end of the first stage of trigger travel. On a very light trigger, this is an advanced skill that takes considerable practice on the range to master, and is not something you should try for the first time out in the field.

Learning to read the movements of the rabbit is not something that you will pick up from a book; it is something that you will only learn by watching rabbits, not with a gun in your hand, but with a pair of binoculars and a notebook. Great hunters are those with a deep interest in animal behaviour, who gain as much pleasure from watching as from shooting, and who will happily stop in the middle of a hunt to sit on a hillside, watching rabbits at play as a buzzard circles high above the warren, screeching as it searches for its next meal.

With many years of such observation behind him, the hunter becomes a part of the countryside in which he hunts, and it is this oneness with nature that makes him such a successful harvester of quarry. It really does not matter how great a shot you are, if you do not cultivate a deep understanding of nature and the animals that you hunt; you can only shoot rabbits if you are able to find them.

Great shooting has a lot to do with the mind: awareness, anticipation, coolness, concentration and visualization are just as important as trigger control and correctly zeroed sights. Awareness and anticipation come through studying nature, so that your mind is programmed with the ways of your quarry. The coolness and concentration are aspects of the self-control required to discipline your mind, so that it does not trigger the detrimental effects caused by excitement.

When the knowledgeable country mind is linked to self-control, you have a very efficient hunter. Add to this the mental skill to visualize the shot (which takes both ballistic knowledge and imagination), and you have the mind of an advanced airgun hunter. When you add to this the physical skills of marksmanship, you have a hunter capable of tackling the most challenging sharpshooting feats it is possible to face in the field.

A FEW NOTES ON PHYSICAL MARKSMANSHIP SKILLS

The most important aspect of marksmanship is the ability to release the shot without transmitting any disturbance from your body to the gun, as the shot travels down and out of the barrel. Such disturbance is the major cause of missed shots with a rifle and scope that have been correctly set up. The main causes of disturbance are a poor trigger pull, or the effect of breathing; fluidity is key to the trigger pull and is the reason why a breath pause has to be employed as the shot is released. Fluidity in the trigger finger requires understanding how the trigger works, and the correct placement of the finger on the trigger, using the finger pad, at the very end of the finger, on the trigger blade.

Use any other part of the finger and the pull will be of a rotational nature, as opposed to straight backwards; pull rotation, no matter how insignificant, obviously shifts the strike point off the intended point of aim.

Fluidity requires feeling, and the best way to develop trigger sensitivity is to dry fire a weapon. If you use PCP fitted with a buddy bottle, you can remove the buddy bottle, as there is no need to discharge air with each dry shot. However, if you do remove it, place a clean plastic bag (the small freezer bags are ideal) over the end of the regulator and tape it in place, so as to prevent dirt or moisture entering into it. Cock and pull the trigger several times before placing the plastic bag over the regulator as it may have some residual air left in it.

With the regulator protected, take the rifle up to your range, cock the rifle, line up the scope onto a target and pull the trigger. No shot will be fired but, even so, you should, through visualization, know where the shot would strike had it been fired. Spend half an hour or so dry firing and you will discover that you get to feel the rhythm of the trigger.

If you think that dry firing a weapon sounds silly, and you doubt the merit of the exercise, then think again; Ed McGivern, one of the world's greatest shots with pistol and rifle, advocates dry firing for the development of feeling and technique. W.E Fairbairn and E.A Sykes, the men responsible for training the commandos and other elite forces

The finger pad on the trigger.

of World War Two, used dry firing as part of their weapons training programme. The special forces snipers of today, such as the American Navy SEAL snipers, also use dry firing to teach the correct manipulation of the trigger, which they consider to be the fundamental skill of marksmanship, around which all the other skills are built. So time spent dry firing is time well spent.

Breath control should also be practised whilst dry firing the weapon. The breath pause should occur when the aim point is precisely fixed on the kill zone of the target. Do not take the breath too early, and do not take an extra deep breath before the pause, but breathe as normal and take the pause at the end of the inhalation stage, holding the breath in a very relaxed manner.

You should hold the breath for a maximum of five seconds, which is more time than is required to make a gentle pull on the trigger to deliver the shot, but it is much better if the breath is only held for a second. This does not sound like a lot of time, but it is possible for a skilled pistol shot to draw a pistol from the holster, raise it to the level aim, and fire two, precisely aimed, shots in 1.5 seconds or less. Therefore, a second for the final trigger pull on a rifle that has been locked onto the target is a huge amount of time.

Though there should be minimal hesitation in the final trigger pull, the initial stage of target engagement – lining up of the aim point on the quarry's kill zone – should not be rushed, but carried out with cool deliberation. Make sure that the alignment is precise and that there is no cant in the rifle, which, if the rifle and scope have been correctly aligned with one another, will be down to poor technique.

There is a very effective way to check the quality of your hold, if you have the rifle set up with a Weaver rail that has a level attached to the end. To test your hold, remove the scope and then, on the range, take up a variety of shooting positions, from the prone to the standing. In each position, aim at a target set at 30yd, using the front of the barrel as the aim point. When you have established your aim on the target do not move anything, other than your eyes, to glance at the level. If you have a good technique, the bubble in the level will be dead centre, but if your technique is poor, the bubble will be off to one side and you know that you need to make a correction to your hold. Corrections to the hold should be made to the rifle with the scope removed, so that you can see what you're doing. Then it is simply a matter of varying the hold until you see the bubble in the level come to the centre.

You will need to spend hours simply bringing the rifle into the hold in the new position, because your muscle memory will want to go into the old position with which it is familiar, and only hours of practice will re-educate it out of its bad habit.

The aiming and delivery of the shot should be one continuous, smooth movement, involving five interlinked processes. These are:

The initial lining up of the aim point on the kill zone of the quarry. This process includes any adjustments made to the turret, to compensate for windage and elevation.

The taking up of the first stage of trigger travel.

The final, precise alignment of the aim point.

The breath pause.

The smooth trigger pull.

If, after five seconds of breath pause, which you should time by counting in your head, the shot has not been made, then resume a normal breathing rhythm, release the pressure on the trigger and go back to stage one. No matter how great the temptation, never take a shot unless you are truly satisfied that every aspect of the shot – from your hold of the rifle, to the precise alignment of the aim point – is as perfect as is humanly possible. If you are not totally satisfied, return to stage one and make the required correction to bring about the necessary level of perfection.

Long-range shooting at ranges of 40 to 45yd is all about being fastidious, to the point of obsession, and it is only when this kind of approach is adopted that you will achieve consistent, clean kills at long range.

Every single long-range shot needs to be taken from a supported position; the rifle must be supported by something, other than the body alone, such as a bipod, a cleft in a tree, the bonnet of a vehicle, or any other such convenient object. The only unsupported position that should ever be used for a long-range shot, if there is no other option, is the kneeling position, with the elbow resting on the raised knee.

MARKSMANSHIP TEST

Sadly, very few hunters spend sufficient time on the range practising their skills and, consequently, they are only moderate marksmen. On a hunt, even on a very successful day, it is unlikely that the hunter will fire more than ten to fifteen shots, which is far too few shots for advanced levels of marksmanship to be achieved.

Dimensions for silhouette targets.

True life measurements

A. Forehead to base of ear 2.5in

B. Nose to cheek 3in

C. Ear 3in

Shaded area = Kill zone

A target shooter will practice five to six times a week, firing 50 to 100 pellets in each session. For the hunter to gain advanced levels of marksmanship an initial investment of three sessions per week, firing 50 to 100 pellets in each session, will be required; this can be reduced to one session per week when the required standard has been reached. To assess your marksmanship, try the following two, very demanding, tests.

1 Cut ten life-size silhouettes of a rabbit's head out of a piece of card and mark the kill zone on each one (the diagram gives the required dimensions).

   Attach each silhouette to a piece of stick, and then set the sticks into the ground at 40yd from your shooting position. Fire three shots at each target. When all ten targets display groupings well within the marked kill zone, measuring 15mm or less, you have achieved the required standard. If just one pellet across the ten targets is off the mark, then you have failed the test. The 15mm groupings are the starting point of advanced marksmanship and you should continue to work at your marksmanship until 12mm groupings appear.

   This, however, is only the first part of test No1. Part two involves setting up five silhouettes at the following ranges: 45yd, 38yd, 35yd and 30yd. Now fire three shots at each target; the required level of marksmanship is achieved when every single target is marked with all three shots, within the kill zone, in groupings of 15mm or less. This is not an easy test by any means, and it may take a considerable amount of practice before you can achieve the required level of marksmanship, but if you are willing to put in the practice then you will get there.

2 Test number two involves marking up a clock face on a piece of card, with a diameter of just 8cm and divided up into eight portions. Place the clock face on a stick, and place the stick in the ground, 40yd from your shooting position. Now, fire one shot into the first portion of the clock, then, working from the twelve in a clockwise direction, place one shot in each of the remaining portions. Then repeat the process, going in an anti-clockwise direction, placing each shot fractionally below the first. When you can produce a pattern on the clock face, like that shown on the above diagram, you have achieved the required level of marksmanship to engage live targets with an air rifle at long range. This second test is a very challenging one, so do not lose heart – it may take six months before you can pull it off.

The clock face.

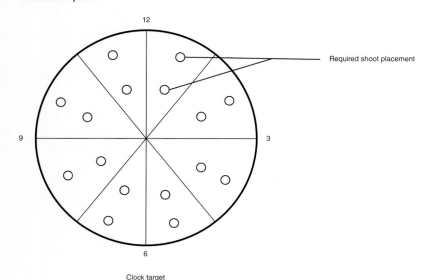

Clock target

Index

RELATED TITLES
FROM CROWOOD

Air Rifle Hunting

JOHN DARLING

ISBN 978 1 85223 063 0
160pp, 85 illustrations

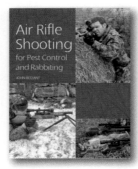

Air Rifle Shooting for Pest Control and Rabbiting

JOHN BEZZANT

ISBN 978 1 84797 043 5
192pp, 140 illustrations

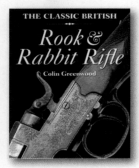

The Classic British Rook and Rabbit Rifle

COLIN GREENWOOD

ISBN 978 1 86126 880 8
200pp, 300 illustrations

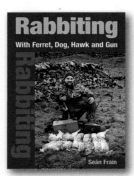

Rabbiting

SEÁN FRAIN

ISBN 978 1 86126 802 0
144pp, 110 illustrations

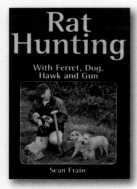

Rat Hunting

SEÁN FRAIN

ISBN 978 1 86126 741 2
144pp, 100 illustrations

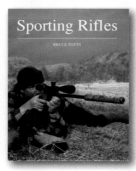

Sporting Rifles

BRUCE POTTS

ISBN 978 1 84797 107 4
224pp, 180 illustrations

In case of difficulty ordering, contact the Sales Office:

The Crowood Press Ltd
Ramsbury
Wiltshire
SN8 2HR
UK

Tel: 44 (0) 1672 520320
enquiries@crowood.com
www.crowood.com